IRISH
MURDERS
—— 2 ——

IRISH MURDERS

2

TERRY PRONE

Additional research by Mary Boyle

POOLBEG

Published in 1994 by
Poolbeg Press Ltd,
Knocksedan House,
123 Baldoyle Industrial Estate,
Dublin 13, Ireland

© Terry Prone 1994

The moral right of the author has been asserted.

A catalogue record for this book is available from the British Library.

ISBN 1 85371 272 8

Cover design by Poolbeg Group Services Ltd
Set by Poolbeg Group Services Ltd in Garamond 10/14
Printed by The Guernsey Press Ltd,
Vale, Guernsey, Channel Islands.

For Lochinvar from The Lady

Terry Prone is author of *Get That Job, Write and Get Paid For It, Just a Few Words, Do Your Own Publicity* and *Be Your Own Boss* (with Frances Stephenson).

Acknowledgements

Sergeant Bill Kelly, Sergeant Pat Kiley and the Staff of the Garda Press Office in the Phoenix Park.

Eamon O'Fiachan, ex-Detective Sergeant in the Ballistics Section, Garda Technical Bureau.

Tony McMahon, ex-Detective Chief Superintendent, Garda Síochána.

The Director and Staff of the National Archives, with special thanks to Gregory O'Connor.

Jimmy McLoughlin, Gilbert Library, Pearse Street.

Joe McFadden, Chief Nursing Officer, Central Mental Hospital, Dundrum.

The willingness with which they gave their time and expertise is very much appreciated.

CONTENTS

YOUNG, GOOD-LOOKING – AND IN THE WRONG PLACE AT THE WRONG TIME

The Murder of Patricia O'Toole

She was young and good-looking. The pictures running in all the newspapers in August 1991 showed her in a white dress, pearls, her hair upswept, with tendrils touching her neck. They were pictures from her wedding, some years previously.

At thirty-one, she had a good job in insurance, a good life, knew how to get the most out of it, and had a sense that all options were open to her. That summer, she and her husband were talking about change. A business venture had failed, and they had put their £70,000 Killiney house on the market to help repay the £29,000 they owed to National Irish Bank. Putting the house on the market got them thinking about getting out of Ireland altogether. It would not have been the first time. Patricia had lived for two years in Greece. Brian had lived in Spain, where he had been married to a Spaniard before he met Patricia. Now, the two discussed going back to Spain or moving to Los Angeles. Patricia favoured Los Angeles, where she could pursue her interest in aerobics – she worked out several times a week at the Friarsland Perfect Fitness Club in Stillorgan. Uh uh, Brian said, pointing to the level of violence in Los Angeles.

The discussion was put on hold, and the couple got on with their work and their extensive social life.

A week later, at the start of a late summer heatwave, Patricia was found after dawn, lying bloodied and dead at the side of Mount Venus Road in the foothills of the Dublin mountains.

Brian hadn't reported to the gardaí the fact that his wife was missing. He had been working as a bouncer in Buck Whaley's nightclub in Leeson Street and, finding the house empty on his return that Friday night, assumed that Patricia had stayed overnight with a friend rather than drive her white Peugeot 205 when over the legal alcohol limit.

When discovered near the canal, the Peugeot had a bloodstained steering wheel, with a clear palmprint etched in blood on it. It also had a clump of Patricia's highlighted hair stuck to the seatbelt bolt on the passenger side.

Patricia herself was lying on a patch of gravel, one of her arms at an impossible angle, her face and body showing all of the evidence of a frenzied attack that had gone on after her death. The gardaí quickly found the main weapon. It was a big black brick. That brick, it would later be established, had been gripped in both hands by Patricia's killer and brought down with manic force on her face, cracking her skull, crushing her nose, pulverising her cheekbones and separating her jaw completely from her skull. She had not been raped.

The gardaí began their investigations by trying to find out who she was. Because she had not been reported missing, this wasn't easy, and there was real fear that the hiatus between the finding of her body and establishing who she was might make the identification of her murderer more difficult.

Once they knew who she was, the task was to trace Patricia's movements the previous night. On 31 August, she had spent the best part of the night at an office party for a colleague who was leaving Consolidated Insurance Brokers in Mount Street, the company where Patricia worked. The party had started in the popular Scruffy Murphy's pub and had moved on to Russell's pub, Patricia in high good humour throughout. The third location for the party was the Pronto Grill in Ranelagh. There, the group had consumed a bottle of wine. The remnants of the insurance office party constituted the last group to leave the Pronto Grill that night. When they parted company, it was about half past one.

After that point it became more difficult to trace Patricia's movements. She had mentioned to some of those involved in the office party that she was going to see a friend. The indications – later – were that she had set off to visit a former boyfriend. Why, nobody will ever know. She never got there.

The gardaí established that she had asked for directions in Inchicore. By painstaking elimination of almost 500 cars, they found a man who had been stopped by Patricia and who had given her street directions.

There, the trail went dead, and the gardaí were forced to embark on a massive broad-spectrum, census-type investigation in the area where the murder victim had last been seen. Patricia's grief-stricken family were left to imagine what had happened to her. Anne Scannell, the dead girl's married sister, even thought that Patricia's husband might, following "some sort of a massive row", have murdered her.

Meanwhile, in another part of the city, on that Saturday

morning, another part of the sad story had started to unravel. Rosaleen Holland was alone in her flat, sleeping late because she had been out late with her boyfriend the night before. At nine o'clock, she woke, looked outside and saw her boyfriend standing against the wall, locked out. She let him in and went back to bed. He undressed and joined her.

Later that day, he laundered some of his clothes in the washing machine. Not very successfully, she thought resentfully, noting that his blue trousers had run into everything else in the load, casting a blueish tinge over the lot. Some of her own clothes had been included. Other than the unsuccessful clothes-washing, there was little of note that weekend for Rosaleen. Nor was the early part of the following working week particularly unusual. Someone mentioned the murder of the blonde insurance worker to her, but because she didn't know her, she didn't react.

"It had nothing to do with me," she said.

She was to be proved tragically wrong one week later. On Monday 9 September, she took a phone call at work from her boyfriend, a soldier named Sean Courtney who had done a tour of duty in the Lebanon. He had something to tell her, he said. That something was important enough for her to leave work at 3 pm, when he came by in his car to collect her. It was a strange journey, the drive back to her flat. Sean was crying. After they arrived he asked her to go back down to the army jeep parked outside and to pull a newspaper out from under the driver's seat but not to look at it.

She collected the paper and went back indoors. On its front page was the big murder story, with Patricia O'Toole's bright face dominating it. Rosaleen now realised that she had known Patricia. Briefly. Very briefly. The insurance worker had stopped Rosaleen and Sean in the street one night at the end of August to ask street directions.

Rosaleen Holland and Sean Courtney had been living together for a few weeks when they went to a disco in the West County Hotel. When the bar was just about to close at 12.30 am, there had been four pints of Carlsberg lined up in front of Courtney. He had downed them all before setting off for a friend's house, where he slept. Later, the couple were walking home when Patricia O'Toole's car pulled up. Courtney started to give directions which, Patricia indicated, she could not follow.

They had both got into the white car with her and eventually Rosaleen had been dropped off while Sean stayed with the driver to make sure she got safely to where she was going.

Recalling all of this, Rosaleen could hear her boyfriend's voice. He was telling her that he had killed the woman after a row in her car.

"I just kept looking at the picture," she later recalled. "I couldn't believe what he was saying to me, that he'd killed the girl."

Courtney told his girlfriend that a row had happened in the white Peugeot between himself and the woman he had known for less than an hour. The details came spilling out, along with the tears. He had picked up a rock and battered her. Torn off her clothes. Driven off, covered in her blood, and parked her car somewhere. The keys he had tossed into the canal.

Having thus submerged his girlfriend in horror, Courtney pulled himself together and went back to work in the army jeep, telling her not to worry. Neither knew that the step-by-step garda investigation was bringing investigators very close to the flat where the couple were living.

Much later that same day, Rosaleen Holland contacted the gardaí, with Sean Courtney's agreement.

"We would have caught him eventually," one of the gardaí later said. But just how long "eventually" would have been, given that the victim and the murderer had no prior contact, is anybody's guess.

Following Rosaleen Holland's phone call, Courtney was arrested at Cathal Brugha Barracks at a quarter to one on the morning of 10 September – exactly ten days after Patricia O'Toole's murder. Taken to Tallaght Garda Station, he said that he did not need a solicitor, and made a statement admitting to killing Patricia after a row with her. He said he had no intention of killing her when he got into the car with her. The confession was elicited and signed during the night.

In daylight, many hours later, the guards accompanied Courtney to various locations to confirm where he'd abandoned the body, left the car, and tossed the keys into the canal. There was no doubt in the detectives' minds that they had their man. They charged him with the murder and he made no response. He was obviously upset and emotional, they noted.

When the case came to trial at the beginning of the following year, Courtney was no longer so emotional. On the contrary, for most of the trial, which he attended in trim uniform, black beret tucked into the epaulette on its right shoulder, he was impassive. Impassive as he listened to State Pathologist Dr John Harbison describe how Patricia had died as a result of inhaling her own blood while unconscious. Impassive as he listened to his own life story told by people who had loved him.

One of those was Amanda Courtney, who had met the young soldier when she was only eighteen. Two years later, she gave birth to their first child, and they got married in 1985. Although Courtney had his faults as a husband and wasn't a great provider, Amanda said that in those early years, they'd had a good relationship. He was fun to be with.

Courtney had always wanted to be an army man, wanting to enlist as soon as he had put his Inter Cert behind him. He had learned sign-writing to fill in the time until he was old enough to join, at which stage he had become a driver with the 2nd Infantry Battalion and had been based in Cathal Brugha Barracks in Dublin.

Then came the first tour of duty with the United Nations Peacekeeping force in the Lebanon, with the 61st battalion. He was gone from April to October 1987, and on his return he and Amanda used the couple of thousand pounds they had saved to fit out a new home in Leighlin Road, Crumlin. Back he went to the Lebanon, this time with the 63rd battalion, in April of the following year. This time he was involved in an incident at a checkpoint where he opened fire on a gunman. He subsequently received threats to his life.

Courtney came home in the summer of 1988 for the birth of his second son. Complications at the birth (the baby was born by Caesarean section and had a hip deformity, later rectified) left him so upset that he was granted an extra fortnight's leave. But even after the extra leave, he didn't want to go back to the Lebanon. However, duty called, and off he went, to return home in October of the same year a changed man, or so the court was told.

Now, according to Amanda, there was no "great fun." Instead, he constantly shouted at her and at the children, and smacked the elder boy very hard. Courtney's mother stopped visiting his home because of the shouting at the children. Amanda suggested he get psychiatric help, but he refused.

In addition, he had terrifying nightmares. In his absence, his wife had taken to sleeping with an axe-handle beside the bed to defend herself if burglars came into the house at night. On one occasion, Courtney's nightmares were so ferocious that he surfaced, screaming and clutching the axe-handle, threatening an unseen and non-existent intruder in the room.

At this point, tours of duty in the Lebanon, starting in April, were something of an unpleasant routine, and Sean Courtney duly set off again in 1990. This time, it took only four days to establish that he was not fit to serve and he was sent home to St Brichin's military hospital, where he was visited by his wife and parents.

"He was crying uncontrollably and walking around in a daze," Amanda later recalled.

On release from hospital, where he had been under psychiatric care, Courtney went home, but moved out after a month. The marriage had died, the final blow delivered when Amanda spotted her husband driving with another woman. One day, Courtney came home, packed his belongings into plastic bags and took off.

Later he moved in with Rosaleen Holland, who said that he had always treated her very well and without violence, but who confirmed that he shouted at her and sometimes cried loudly in his sleep. She, too, suggested psychiatric help. Not long afterwards came the night when Patricia O'Toole was murdered.

There was no question that Courtney was the man who killed Patricia. Forensic scientist Dr Maureen Smith testified that she had examined clothes owned by Courtney and found bloodstains on a tie that matched Patricia O'Toole's blood. The bloody palmprint found on the steering wheel of the dead woman's car matched the print of Courtney's left hand.

The main question centred on Courtney's frame of mind that August night.

His family made it clear that he had returned from his third tour of duty in the Lebanon a deeply changed and troubled man, who had needed three months of psychiatric care in St Brichin's hospital. Senior Council Patrick MacEntee, a legendary figure among Dublin's most prominent barristers, suggested to the court that Courtney was insane at the time he killed Patricia because he was suffering from Post-Traumatic Stress Disorder and this had prevented him from refraining from the violent act. Post-Traumatic Stress Disorder is a term that gained currency in the years following the Vietnam War, when some men who had done their tour of duty had returned to the United States where they failed to maintain normal relationships, lost jobs one after another, and, on occasion, were involved in alcohol- and substance-abuse and in violence.

Courtney's girlfriend had testified that alcohol exacerbated his tendency to be violent, and had indicated that on the night of the murder he had drunk perhaps a dozen pints of beer. Not only did alcohol make Courtney more violent, the girlfriend admitted, it also made him tell his life story to anybody who would listen. Whether he had done this with Patricia O'Toole was never clear.

Senior Counsel MacEntee quoted Courtney's own evidence that, while he was talking to Patricia O'Toole in the car, she had asked him about himself, and, when he was telling her, had interrupted him. "You never know who you are picking up at this time of night," he had her saying. "I could get you done for attacking me. It's your word against mine . . . "

This Courtney had interpreted as a threat and, lashing out, he had struck her almost as a reflex action. She had slumped in the seat, and Courtney had driven the car without any sense of where he was going. At a certain point, Patricia had regained consciousness and – understandably – started to scream. At this point, Courtney panicked and killed her.

MacEntee interpreted the initial blow as a response to a threat created in Courtney's mind by his Post-Traumatic Stress Disorder. The Senior Counsel then quoted State Pathologist John Harbison's evidence that Patricia's body showed evidence of an attack of enormous intensity, viciousness and frequency. All of this, he proposed, added up to a picture of a man who was simply not in control.

For the State, Peter Charleton, BL, said that Courtney was sane at the time of the killing and had intended to kill Patricia.

"It is not and never has been a defence in law that a person's capacity to control their actions is diminished," he said.

He went further. If Courtney was suffering from Post-Traumatic Stress Disorder, then the most likely cause was the murder of Mrs O'Toole.

It might well be true, the State conceded, that some kind of overwhelming anger hit Courtney as a result of something Patricia had said to him, and that he had struck her at the five-roads junction in Inchicore, causing her to slump unconscious.

But he then drove a long way with an unconscious person on the seat beside him to a location where he beat her to death. That pattern of action made it "impossible to make a formulation of no intent." In other words, it was claimed, Courtney had taken Patricia to the foothills of the Dublin mountains with malice aforethought.

After eight hours of closing speeches and briefings from Mr Justice Kevin Lynch, the five-woman, seven-man jury retired. According to journalist Senan Molony, writing in the *Daily Star* of the following morning, they reached the sparsely furnished jury room at about 7.30 pm. The heating had gone off earlier and the room was already starting to get cold. The cold air rapidly filled with smoke as the ten smoking members of the jury lit up. Car keys were handed to an usher with the request that jurors' cars be moved out of car parks which were about to close; a signal read by those outside that the jurors were expecting a long hard night's work.

The jury set to work, analysing the evidence which had been placed before them. When it came to making the decision as to whether or not Courtney was insane, the jury was unanimous in deciding that he was sane. Half an hour after midnight, they had come to a decision.

In the meantime, few people had left the courtroom. To fill in the time, there was gossip, chat and the occasional burst of tension-relieving laughter. Patricia's widowed father was furious at the latter.

"You are all laughing, but Pat is not laughing," he shouted. "Pat is dead."

By a majority verdict of ten to two, the jury finally found Courtney guilty. All hell broke loose in the courtroom. Friends of Patricia cheered. Courtney's family moaned. His girlfriend, who had said she planned to stand by him, wept.

Justice Lynch then sentenced Private Courtney to the mandatory life sentence. When the judge left the courtroom, Courtney's stolid passivity disappeared.

"She was only a fucking tramp," he suddenly yelled, to be quieted by those close to him, while Patricia's relatives grimly noted the lack of remorse implicit in the yell.

He was moved to a high-security prison, where he was visited by his parents and by his girlfriend. She should, he told her, stop brooding about him and get on with her life.

Five days later, Courtney was in court again, to hear his application for leave to appeal rejected, on the grounds that the verdict had been absolutely correct and that it would be "radical, far-reaching, dangerous and wrong" to agree that he deserved an appeal hearing.

But the refusal of leave to appeal was not the end of the case. There was much discussion of the claim to Post-Traumatic Stress Disorder, with the army stating bluntly that so few Irish soldiers have ever been identified as suffering from it that to even publish the numbers would be ridiculous. In the last few years, the army pointed out, only about seventy-eight soldiers have had to be brought back to Ireland from an overseas tour of duty, and roughly sixty-eight of them were physically injured in some way. Only about ten were diagnosed as suffering from mental health problems, all of them (like Courtney) received hospital treatment on their return, and had psychiatric help made available to them.

Whatever about the army treatment of their men, the treatment of insanity by the law was severely criticised following the Courtney case. Noting that the Programme for Government published by the incoming Fianna Fail/Labour partnership included proposals for the introduction of a verdict of "diminished responsibility" which would have the effect of reducing the charge of murder to manslaughter, one senior counsel observed that this defence has existed in England since 1957 and would allow a defence of impaired responsiblity in O'Toole's case.

What angered many people, particularly women, was the concentration on the victim and her lifestyle. One night in her life was taken in sharp focus and allowed to suggest both that she had a "free and easy" lifestyle and that she had in some way caused her own murder. There was angry reaction to suggestions that a woman out on her own that late at night, asking directions from strangers and allowing a man into the car with her, was "asking for trouble." The director of the Dublin Rape Crisis Centre pointed out that it made no sense to suggest that women should stay at home to ensure that they were never attacked. Patricia's sister, Anne, went further.

"All she had done was to go out for a few drinks with a few pals from work and then decide to call around to a friend of hers. People are not going to tolerate the streets of Dublin being made a no-go area for women at night."

Crime reporters remembered the deaths of a number of women who had found themselves the victim of random violence in broad daylight. They recalled cases such as that of Nurse Bridie Gargan (see *Irish Murders I*), attacked by a total stranger in the middle of the day in Phoenix Park.

The fact that Private Courtney was allowed to wear his army uniform throughout the trial galled many people. The rules have since been changed, so that it is now against army regulations for defendants to wear uniforms to trials where they are charged with criminal offences unless directed to do so by an official order.

A week after that new ruling came into effect, Courtney himself was discharged from the army by the Minister for Defence and the Marine, Mr David Andrews, TD, on the basis that Courtney had "admitted committing a serious offence on 31 August, 1991."

It was left to Brian O'Toole to sum up the whole sad case.

"Patricia was in the wrong place at the wrong time. Five minutes later and she would be alive today. The hardest thing for me is to wake up in the morning and face another day and she isn't there."

"I Don't Think I Will
Hang for It . . . "

A Murder in Mayo

Generation after generation, children hear the same message: "Don't go with strangers." These days, there are even training courses to prepare youngsters to reject the plausible but unknown newcomer – as if sexual abuse and murder were only done by wild-eyed new arrivals to a community.

The reality is otherwise. Very often, sexual abuse is suffered by children who know their abuser and who therefore assume that what he is doing to them is OK. Murder, too, whether of adults or of children, is most often committed by individuals who know the victim well.

In the case of young Michael Loftus, there was no suspicion at the beginning of "criminal interference" or of murder. The eight-and-a-half-year-old boy went missing on a Sunday in June 1945. He was last seen at about half-eleven that morning, and by lunchtime, his family members were out and about, asking local people if they'd come across him. As dusk fell, Michael's father, now seriously worried because his son hadn't come home, told the local gardaí at the station in Crossmolina, County Mayo, that his son was missing. A search swung into action, with the

15

gardaí, helped by civilians, going through the area to find any traces of the missing boy.

The search lasted a week that must have been agony for the boy's family. On Monday the twenty-fifth, eight days after the disappearance, it was the child's own father who spotted a patch of loosely packed earth under a furze bush in a field. Sick at heart, the father showed the area to the searching gardaí and asked them to investigate. They did. The loosely packed earth covered the shallow grave of Michael Joseph Loftus, who lay face-down under two feet of soil, fully dressed and grievously traumatised in the area of the head.

Whoever had done the digging had run out of energy for the task, for the grave was not big enough, so that the legs were bent at the knees and the feet were slightly higher than the rest of the body.

The child's body was removed with a minimum of disturbance and taken to the town of Crossmolina, where a full post-mortem examination was begun by Dr MA Kehoe at 10.35 that night. Meanwhile, the gardaí resumed their search of the surrounding fields, this time looking for any items forgotten by the murderer which might help them identify him. Extra gardaí were drafted in to help.

About 500 yards away from the shallow grave, the searchers came upon a pair of men's boots, which they left in place in the hedge where they had been found, retiring to observation points from which they could see, but not be seen. Night fell. Just after midnight, a figure was seen to move in the darkness, quietly coming to within a few yards of the boots. "Walking cautiously and in a crouching attitude," was how the gardaí described him. They promptly emerged from concealment about seven yards away, and introduced themselves to the figure, who turned out to be a twenty-nine-year-old neighbour of the Loftuses, Stephen Murphy. Murphy was a loner who was regarded as peculiar. On this night, however, he claimed to have been looking for a stray bullock.

"I hope you have no suspicion of me," he said anxiously.

"Why do you say that?" asked the gardaí.

"I thought you were following me."

They were, but now, ostensibly, took his explanation on board and let him go, keeping him under observation.

At around about seven o'clock on the following evening, they noticed Murphy on the move again, this time to an old fort quite near his father's farm. But if they noticed Murphy, Murphy also noticed them, and took to his heels with some enthusiasm. This greatly enhanced the investigators' interest in him, and they chased him. When they caught up with him, he was rattled and excited, telling Garda O'Connell, who had outpaced him, that he had hidden a pair of trousers in the fort.

Go get the trousers, suggested Garda O'Connell. At first, Murphy refused, then changed his mind, finding and handing over the trousers before returning to his father's house, supervised by Garda O'Connell, who sent word to the garda in charge of the investigation that the dead boy had one neighbour who was behaving oddly and who might be worth a visit.

Murphy's home was now visited by a Chief Superintendent, a Superintendent, and a detective, who were told, on their arrival, that Murphy wanted to talk to them. He was duly cautioned, and began to talk, telling the gardaí that he lived with his father and his brother, and had known the dead boy since he was a child.

"He used call to my father's house on an average about once a fortnight, and sometimes once a week," he told them.

The last time he had seen the child, he said, was on the previous Friday week, two days before the youngster had gone missing. The first he had heard of the problem was, he said, at lunchtime on the Sunday, when his father and young Mikie's father, Josie Loftus, had met in the street and had been joined by Stephen. Loftus asked Stephen Murphy if he had seen Mikie.

"I said I didn't," Stephen Murphy told the gardaí. "There was nothing further said."

Stephen Murphy then went into his home, tidied up after lunch and – as he often did – sat down to read on his own. Mid-afternoon, he was visited by one of Josie Loftus's workmen.

"He asked me if Mikie was around the place at all," Stephen recalled. "I told him he wasn't."

The workman went away, and Stephen continued to read. It was strange behaviour for an active young man who not only had known the missing child for years, but been quite close to him, and who now could be in no doubt that some pretty intensive searching was going on. It was not until late afternoon that Stephen Murphy put his novel to one side and joined the searchers, starting with a visit to the Loftus home. The boy's mother looked at the new addition to the search team.

"Well, Stephen," she said. "I wonder where Mikie could have gone to."

Stephen made no comment, and drew no inference of special knowledge on his part. He went off and searched along the river, later joining the main search party, led by the local sergeant. Days, dates, encounters and minutiae poured out of Stephen in such a torrent as simultaneously to present him as an unlikely suspect and as a strange, cold and clever man who could tailor his language to minimise his association with the dead boy.

Murphy was known to be keen on ferreting, a sport always more popular in Britain than in Ireland, which has almost died out in the decades since the murder. Ferreting entails putting a ferret down a hole to catch a rabbit, or under floorboards to sort out rats. In his detailed statement to the gardaí, he quite gratuitously – it seemed – told them that he had never taken anyone with him when engaging in this sport.

"Did you ever take young Loftus with you ferreting?" asked one of the gardaí.

"I never took him with me," Murphy said. "He came with me twice as far as I remember . . . "

Regular trips, instigated by Murphy, suddenly became two half-remembered occasions where the eight-and-a-half-year-old had just tagged along.

"I do not agree that the little boy was more attached to me than to any other person outside his parents," he added.

The only thing that didn't fit neatly into Stephen Murphy's explanation of life, the universe and everything, was why he should have been hiding a pair of trousers in a long-abandoned fort. They weren't even *his* trousers, he explained. He had found them in an unoccupied dwelling house on a neighbouring farm. The last time he had worn them was on the Sunday the Loftus boy had disappeared. No, he assured the investigators, there was nothing else in the fort. The gardaí allowed as how they'd just check that out themselves, thank you very much all the same, Stephen. He accompanied the gardaí to the fort and retrieved four items of his clothing. Suspiciously stained, that clothing. But again, Stephen had a ready explanation. Or two. Or three. The stains were probably grease. Or if they weren't grease; if they were bloodstains, then they were his own bloodstains, probably created when he rubbed his hands on them having been scratched by briars.

In fact, the stains were a lot more incriminating than a little blood from briar scratches, but that emerged later.

As the gardaí were talking to Stephen Murphy, some information had already emerged from the post-mortem examination of the dead boy. There was blood on the child's right wrist and on the cuff of his tweedy jacket. The palm and wrist of his left hand were bloodstained, and there was bloodstaining on the shins, calves and knees. The child's head had suffered truly horrific damage, with extensive fracturing to the back of the skull.

The gaping fractures left an opening seven-and-a-half inches long, running virtually from ear to ear, and there were other gaps in the child's skull, with the bone fragments driven inwards. The child had died of shock produced by multiple severe injuries to the skull causing laceration of the brain. The injuries were of the kind which would be produced by several violent blows from a heavy instrument such as a spade.

The newspapers were predicting an early arrest; a prediction which seemed to fill Stephen Murphy with dread. He asked one of the policemen if much evidence would be needed before they arrested someone.

"It all depends on the evidence on hand," the garda

responded, in a masterly example of solid non-communication.

"A fellow could easily be pulled into a thing like this and be convicted in the wrong," Murphy opined.

Later that same day, he was more specific in his identification of the "fellow who could easily be pulled into a thing like this." The "fellow" was now himself.

"I'm going to be arrested tonight," he predicted to a neighbour named Patrick Cadden. "The guards are after me."

"What for?" the neighbour inquired. "For the killing of young Mikie Loftus," came the answer.

"Somebody gave away on me," Stephen said, obscurely.

But, asked the neighbour, had Stephen actually killed the child? A quick denial came from the twenty-nine-year-old.

"If I got a bicycle I would clear away from them," he added.

"Where can you go?" asked the neighbour, realistically. "Won't they get you anyway? Why don't you stand your ground if you say you did not kill him and not be running away?"

The gardaí did not hang about. On the evening of the twenty-seventh, ten days after young Mikie had gone missing, Stephen Murphy was charged with his murder, and indicated that he did not want to make a statement. A day later, he changed his mind, making a statement wherein he admitted killing the youngster by hitting him over the head with a spade. The spade he had then thrown into the River Deal.

In setting out to search the river, the gardaí were greatly helped by a clever Heath Robinson-type gadget dreamed up by a local garda, Sergeant McGuckian. He took the top and bottom off a tin can, removed the contents, and stuck a round piece of glass into the can where the bottom had been. This rudimentary snorkel allowed searchers to peer into the water and see objects on the bed of the river.

The tin can device quickly revealed a spade-head which was recovered from the river and matched with a spade handle found in the undergrowth of the field where Michael Loftus's grave had been located. Despite its immersion in the river, the spade head was covered in clay, underneath which was found a heavy staining of human blood. To whom did the spade belong? To a local farmer. It had gone missing. Any connection with Stephen Murphy? Murphy had occasionally been employed at the farm from which the instrument had disappeared.

The gardaí were now convinced they had their man, but less clear about what kind of man he was. In prison, he seemed to be clear, cool and in control, telling a fellow prisoner that although he had killed the child, it had not been premeditated.

"I don't think I will hang for it, in any case," he remarked.

To another prisoner, he indicated that the death had been accidental. Examination of the child's body had decisively ruled out that option. The child's head had not suffered one accidental blow, but had been bludgeoned with the spade at least six and probably seven times. What the child's body also revealed was that Mikie had been sexually used by someone over a considerable period of time: "At least many months," was how the trial judge was later to sum it up. "Criminal interference" was how the gardaí described it. "Buggery" was how the medical men described it. One way or the other, the act had been committed on the child's body perhaps a hundred times. No seminal fluid was found on the body, but that, said the state pathologist, was not unexpected. Even if there had been a sexual act shortly before the boy's death, any seminal fluid would have disappeared within a day or so. Seminal stains were found on the trousers taken from Stephen Murphy.

When the case came to court in November of the same year, evidence was given that Mikie had been constantly around Stephen Murphy, accompanying him on trips to snare rabbits. The boy had been seen on the handlebars of Murphy's bike on the day before the murder. So Stephen's denial of a close relationship with the child did not hold up.

His counsel wasted no time on unproductive denial of a relationship which clearly had been close and sexually exploitative. Nor was there any speculation as to how an eight-year-old could become so enslaved by a man nearly twenty years his senior as to tolerate such sexual exploitation over a period of time. The main thrust of the defence case was that Stephen Murphy was not responsible for his actions, because he was insane.

Eminent mental health specialists of the day gave their opinion that the accused was suffering from "dementia praecox." This was described as "an invidious disease of the mind which grew progressively worse and manifested itself in sudden outbursts."

Dementia praecox (dementia of early life) was the name given, at the end of the last century, to a group of diseases which had, up to then, been regarded as separate, but which are now seen as sub-types of schizophrenia.

Schizophrenia tends to be diagnosed when patients are in their late teens or early twenties, although families of patients sometimes suggest that the onset of the disease can be traced back to their observation of their young relative as "always different in some way," or "a loner."

Dr E Fuller Torrey, a clinical and research psychiatrist specialising in schizophrenia, who has written a book on the subject called *Surviving Schizophrenia: A Family Manual* (New York, 1988), says that patients who are likely to respond best to treatment are those who seemed to be fairly normal prior to the onset of the disease.

"Thus, if as children they were able to make friends with others, did not have major problems with delinquency and achieved success levels in school reasonable for their intelligence level, their outcome is likely to be good," he says. "Conversely, if they are described by relatives as 'always a strange child,' had major problems in school or with their peers, were considered delinquent, or were very withdrawn, they are more likely to fall into the poor outcome group."

On the witness stand, Stephen Murphy's father innocently characterised his son as having a poor chance of recovery. Not only did he portray him as being deeply withdrawn, but, long before the publication of research indicating that schizophrenia patients with the best chance of recovery are those who have no history of schizophrenic relatives, Mr Murphy gave the court a sad litany of relatives who were mentally ill. An uncle had died at twenty-seven, so weak-minded that he could not read nor write, and had been unable to dress himself without assistance. Two first cousins had "been in the asylum" and another "had gone silly and used wander." Most significantly, the eldest

24

brother of the accused, dead about ten years, had also been "weak-minded."

Dr John Dunne, the psychiatrist then in charge of Grangegorman and Portrane mental hospitals, said that in view of this grim family history, it was his opinion that if Murphy had committed the crime, he had done it while in such a state of mind as not to realise what he was doing or that it was wrong. Dementia praecox, Dunne told the court, was a disease characterised by a general withdrawal from the realities of life. Dr Dunne agreed that Murphy's statement to the gardaí had no sign of cloudiness or loss of memory about it, but was "cleverly and intelligently exculpatory." He further agreed that it was possible that the spade had been brought to the scene of the crime for the express purpose of doing away with the little boy, but this premeditation would not alter his view that Murphy had been suffering from dementia praecox, a mental illness now called schizophrenia, defined at the time as "often recognised during or shortly after adolescence but frequently in later maturity characterised by disorientation, loss of contact with reality, splitting of the personality."

In the years since Stephen Murphy's trial, there has been much public concern and controversy about links between schizophrenia and violence. Whenever publicity is given to a violent act committed by a schizophrenic, people add two and two together and come up with six: that *all* schizophrenics are violent. This is simply not true. Most schizophrenics are never violent, and those who might be, if properly cared for and medicated, need never be a danger to themselves or anyone else.

Murphy was not portrayed in court as having been previously violent, but as having taken very little interest in anything, never speaking except to answer questions, wanting above all to be left alone.

The medical evidence suggesting insanity did not confine itself to Murphy's brain. "On the contrary," said Dr McCarthy, RMS, the man in charge of Ballinasloe Mental Hospital. (RMS is a discontinued term meaning Resident Medical Superintendent, who was the doctor in charge of both the administrative and medical side of a hospital.) The psychiatrist, who said he had eleven years' experience of dealing with dementia praecox patients, had examined the prisoner in Mountjoy and "found certain physical deformities" in him which were described as "physical stigmata associated with mental disease." These included deformities of his ears, a highly arched "defective" palate, and a drooping of the left eyelid. Add these deformities, mute evidence of mental degeneration, to the evidence given by Murphy's father of a family history of mental illness, and, said the doctor, it would be "next to impossible" for Murphy to have been normal.

In a pattern of interpretation calculated to enrage the modern gay community, paedophilia was not separated from homosexuality.

Not only that, but at least one of the psychiatrists said that he believed all cases of homosexuality were associated with some form of mental derangement.

One way or the other, said the psychiatrists, Murphy may well have known what he was doing, but he didn't know that what he was doing was wrong.

Murphy's first trial ended after the jury had spent only three hours coming to the conclusion that he was guilty. He was sentenced to death. After an appeal, however, the judgement was quashed, and on retrial, Murphy was found "guilty but insane."

The "guilty but insane" verdict has a long history. In seventeenth-century England, a manual for British jurists advised: "If one that is *non compos mentis*, or an idiot, kills a man, this is no felony, for they have not knowledge of Good and Evil, nor can have a felonious intent, nor a will or mind to do harm."

In Britain and Ireland in the following two centuries, much was made of the "wild beast test," which held that when men or women act like wild beasts, they can't be held accountable for a crime. Sir Edward Coke, regarded as one of the founders of British common law, defined murder thus: "When a person of sound memory and discretion unlawfully killeth any reasonable creature in being, and under the king's peace, with malice aforethought, either express or implied."

This definition gave way to the M'Naghton rules in the middle of the nineteenth century. These rules were drawn up as the result of the murder by Daniel M'Naghton of the man who served as Private Secretary to Sir Robert Peel.

For several years, M'Naghton had been labouring under the delusion that he was the victim of injustice at the hands of Sir Robert, who therefore, in M'Naghton's deluded thinking, deserved to be shot. He then mistook the Private Secretary for Sir Robert and shot him dead. He was found guilty but insane, and from his name came the rules which hold that an accused is not responsible if he "was labouring under such a defect of reason, from disease of the mind, as not to know the nature and the quality of the act he was doing, or if he did know it, that he did not know he was doing what was wrong."

Under both British and Irish interpretation of the

M'Naughton rules, the onus is on the defendant to prove insanity, following the report of the House of Lords which drew up the rules, and which stated: "We submit our opinion to be that the jury ought to be told in all cases that every man is to be presumed to be sane and to possess a sufficient degree of reason to be responsible for his crimes, until the contrary be proved to their satisfaction . . . "

So, not only is the accused assumed to be innocent until proven guilty, but he or she is also assumed to be sane until they prove otherwise.

The situation surrounding Stephen Murphy's case was confused. He had been a bright student at school, but had no ambitions or career drive. He steered clear of relationships. Those who interviewed him in prison found him of "flat affect;" he was expressionless, uninvolved and uninterested. He didn't seem to know that homosexuality was a major criminal offence. He had attacked the child in a way which suggested he had suddenly lost all control, yet had buried him and joined the search party. His comments about "not hanging for it" were indicative of a mind capable of cool analysis of his chances.

The second trial of Stephen Murphy was in the spring of the following year, when a jury found him "guilty but insane" and he was committed to Dundrum Criminal Lunatic Asylum. Dundrum, which has housed so many of Ireland's mentally ill killers, was the first criminal lunatic asylum in these islands. It opened in 1850, almost a century before Broadmoor.

FLEMING – THE NORTHSIDE PLAYBOY

A Marital Triangle that Ended in Death

It was a case of boy meets girl. Almost. The boy was maybe a bit long in the tooth, at thirty-two, for the girl, who was just eighteen. But, small details like that aside, it was romantic enough. John Fleming was an assistant in a draper's shop, a neat man with a lot of wavy dark hair rising off his forehead. Originally from Tuam, he had been apprenticed to a Claremorris draper when he was thirteen and a half. Later, he had spent time in Australia, returning to Ireland convinced he could do better for himself in his home country, and landed himself a job in Hickeys of North Earl Street.

Rita Murtagh was a Dubliner, eldest of a family of seven, working in the Central Café in D'Olier Street when, in 1928, she met John Fleming. He came to the café for lunch every day but Wednesday. Fleming was not a man to rush things, so it took twelve months of growing friendship between the pair before he invited her out, in October, 1929. It was all very pleasant, the courting. He would take her to the pictures, the theatres and to restaurants. Occasionally they would go to places like Whitehall for a companionable walk.

In January, 1930, Fleming took Miss Murtagh to his

home in Carlingford Road, to show her over the house they would share when married. A wedding had been discussed before this visit to the dwelling which was then occupied, Fleming said, by himself and his aunt.

Now, the only problem with this love story is that Fleming was more than a little married. He had been joined in holy wedlock with Ellen, a woman at least thirteen years older than he was, in 1921. Ellen continued to work, and although they had a baby, the child died. Later, Ellen's nephew came to live with them. The Flemings seemed to be a quiet happy family who got on well with their neighbours.

It was one of those neighbours, Mrs O'Rourke from next door at number fifty, who was called to help at midnight on the last day of March, 1932. Ellen Fleming's nephew, John Berry, asked her to come and help, because his aunt was very ill.

Mrs O'Rourke was next door in minutes, asking John Fleming what was wrong with Ellen. A stroke, he thought. Even before climbing the stairs, Mrs O'Rourke could hear Ellen moaning in bed. When she went into the bedroom, Ellen was in considerable distress with, among other problems, intense cramping in her legs and arms. But the sufferer had an explanation for what ailed her which was quite different from that of her husband.

"My husband tried to poison me," she told Mrs O'Rourke, asking the next-door neighbour to send Mr O'Rourke for a doctor. However, John Fleming, apparently eager to help solve his wife's agonising problems, said he would get a doctor and immediately departed in search of one. It was almost one in the morning when he came back, defeated. He had not been able to find one.

The cast of characters widened a little at this point. Mrs O'Rourke had a brother-in-law staying with her at the time. Patrick O'Rourke was on holidays from his job, which, by coincidence, was a nursing post. A minority of Irish nurses have always been men, most of them working in psychiatric hospitals, where it was perceived in the past that their strength was necessary for overcoming frenzied patients in the days before greater chemical control of manic outbreaks. O'Rourke had started his nursing career with Britain's Royal Army Medical Corps and was both a qualified nurse and a "compounder," so he was qualified both to interpret symptoms and to compound medicines.

O'Rourke now arrived in the Fleming's small red-brick two-storey house, where he observed that Ellen was suffering severe muscular cramps all over, even in her neck and jaws. The pain was extreme, and O'Rourke turned to John Fleming and indicated that a doctor had to be found, and found fast. Obediently, off went Fleming into the darkness outside. Back he came, a half-hour later, with another tale of woe. There had, he said, been no response at the doctor's house.

Ellen Fleming was now thirsty, as well as pained and frightened. When she asked for something to drink, her husband obligingly prepared a drink for her. She tasted it. And spat.

"Oh, Jack. That's bitter," she protested. "Like what you gave me in the chocolate."

Her husband gently told her it was just milk and water.

"Drink some of it yourself if it's milk and water," she snapped.

"There may be aspirin in it," he amended weakly, but this drew Mrs O'Rourke on him.

"How could aspirin get into it?" she demanded. "I have the bottle of aspirin in my pocket."

O'Rourke took the glass to examine it, but at that moment, Ellen Fleming again went into spasm, and he ditched the glass on the most convenient nearby surface while he attended to her. When he looked around again, the glass had disappeared and John Fleming likewise.

At this stage, it seemed, Fleming had got a move on and gone in search of a doctor for the third time that eventful night.

Third time lucky? On the contrary. This time it took only twenty minutes to defeat him, and he was back, yet again, now clutching a small glass which he promoted as containing whiskey and port wine to help his wife. Ellen may have been in acute pain, but her brain was working apace. The drink couldn't be whiskey and port wine, she told her husband, for the very good reason that the house held neither form of alcohol.

"Take it away," she gasped. "I will not drink it."

Fleming took the rejected drink away, threw it into the kitchen sink and carefully rinsed out the glass before putting it away. Meanwhile, the trained nurse on holiday was becoming incredulous at the amazing dearth of doctors in the capital.

"It's peculiar that you can't get a doctor in this city of Dublin," Patrick O'Rourke observed acidly to Fleming. "I can get one in half an hour in Connemara."

Lest Fleming be in any doubt about O'Rourke's judgement of the situation, the visitor stated it clearly. "I will hold you responsible for anything that happens to Mrs Fleming," he told Fleming.

Another nurse lived nearby, and Patrick O'Rourke

decided that she was the next best thing to a doctor, so he sent Ellen Fleming's nephew to fetch her. Nurse McDonagh arrived within ten minutes, some time before four in the morning, and began to minister to Ellen, who, at that stage, was beginning to show signs of recovery. The male nurse left the house and went back to bed next door.

As the dawn broke, O'Rourke faced a problem. His holidays were over, and he had to head to Galway. But he was still concerned about his sister-in-law's neighbour. So he dropped in to number forty-eight to see her, and to take Nurse McDonagh aside. He told her he suspected that Ellen was the victim of attempted strychnine poisoning, (of which he had seen other examples in the course of his work) and asked her to make sure that a doctor was called in and told the whole story.

During the morning, there was a replay of the previous night's events, to the extent that the nurse told John Fleming to go and get a doctor. What was different was that this time, Fleming managed to bring a doctor back with him – their GP. The nurse detailed the symptoms, which matched those of strychnine poisoning.

As a method of poisoning, strychnine has a long history. Cleopatra, before she settled on an asp as the ideal method of suicide, looked into the possibilities of poisoning by means of ingestion of the dog button plant, *Strychnos nuxvomica*, from which strychnine is extracted. The queen organised her own clinical trials, dosing her slaves to watch the resultant symptoms, and rejected strychnine because although it was fast-acting, it induced convulsions which left the face grossly distorted after death.

Strychnine is a colourless, crystalline powder with a bitter taste, which, when swallowed, attacks the central nervous system and causes exacerbated reflex effects, so that all of the muscles contract at the same time, starting with stiffness in the neck and face and moving on to spasms of the legs and arms. The spasms worsen, until the victim is arched in agony, feet and head on the ground, but the rest of the body raised off the floor. A touch or a sound or a sudden brightness will all trigger muscle spasms.

The symptoms of strychnine poisoning are quite like those of tetanus, and the body reacts quickly, often about ten minutes after the administration of the poison. Famous murders committed using strychnine were those of four London prostitutes in the nineteenth century at the hands of Chicago man Dr Thomas Neill Cream, and a French murder in 1924. The latter was the slaying of a lover's husband by a middle-aged Frenchman named Vaquier, who dosed the husband with the strychnine mixed into an indigestion remedy. The victim, who died quickly, had much the same reaction to the initial drink as had Ellen Fleming: "My God, it is bitter . . . "

Strychnine and its effects became well known with the rising popularity of detective novels. Agatha Christie's first novel, *The Mysterious Affair at Styles*, centred upon a strychnine murderer who put the poison into his victim's evening hot chocolate. Generally, strychnine as a method of homicide appears more often in fiction than in real life.

One of the peculiarities of the toxin is that doses less than those necessary to cause acute poisoning will produce no symptoms; indeed, strychnine has been used as an ingredient in some medicines. So Ellen Fleming was lucky to survive, and O'Rourke (as was proven by information later emerging about the purchase of strychnine by her husband) was showing good judgement in his diagnosis.

However, the local doctor thought differently. Ellen Fleming, he decided, was suffering from nerves and needed a tonic! That the patient didn't brain the medic at this point says volumes about the times in which they lived. Although she was a mature, bright career woman who must have known that the agony she had suffered the previous night could not by any stretch of the medical imagination be justly attributed to "nerves," she obediently started taking the tablets – or, more precisely, the tonic.

Nurse McDonagh went away, absorbing the diagnosis and another piece of surprising information. Overhearing a conversation between the doctor and John Fleming, she heard the patient's husband tell the doctor that he, Fleming, had known damn well what was wrong with Ellen the previous night, and so he had only pretended to go for the doctor.

Nobody reported any of this to the police. If someone had outlined the details to the gardaí, there is an overwhelming likelihood that they would have interpreted it as a deliberate attempt by Fleming to kill his wife.

Forewarned, the gardaí might have prevented a later murder and the subsequent execution. But O'Rourke was on his way back to Galway, McDonagh had only been there for part of the night, the sick woman was recovering, and John Fleming was at his calm, helpful best. So, in the immediate aftermath of the all-night drama, the neat house in Drumcondra reverted to suburban marital peace, and the neighbours assumed that all was well between the Flemings.

Meanwhile, Fleming and his Central Café girlfriend were becoming closer and closer, more and more intimate. Young Rita wanted to be married, and John Fleming had indicated that this was very much on the cards. When Rita was miserable in hospital in March, 1932, having had her tonsils out, John visited her and promised they'd tie the knot as soon as his "aunt" moved out of Carlingford Road. Not only was his aunt going to leave the house, but, coincidentally, John Berry (who, remember, was actually his wife's nephew) was going to get a job which provided its own living accommodation.

Fleming had taken Rita's virginity – no small sacrifice for a single girl in Dublin of the 1930s – and, like any woman in her vulnerable position, she was highly sensitive to shifts in the balance of their relationship. Prior to 1932, it had been Fleming who had constantly talked of marriage. Then, in 1932, they were "intimate" as often as circumstances permitted. From that time onwards, as she sadly observed, it was Rita who talked marriage, and John who agreed, but somehow never managed to walk her up the aisle.

The new year (1933) brought the revelation to the draper's assistant that he was to become a father. Not by his wife, but by his girlfriend, who was now frantic to be married. No problem, he said; this would happen very quickly. He had always looked forward to fatherhood.

As earnest of his good intentions, he took Rita to a jeweller's shop – Bensons in O'Connell Street – on 6 February. There an assistant named David Ginsberg helped the couple as they examined and eventually selected wedding and engagement rings. The rings chosen were slightly too big for Rita's slender third finger, and so Ginsberg entered in his day-book a description of the rings and of their size. This would facilitate the reduction of the two rings.

Ginsberg asked the "groom-to-be" for a surname, and

thought he heard "Lemming." He repeated it aloud and got no correction, so entered it on the form. He then asked for a deposit. Fleming demurred, undertaking to pay the full amount when he collected the altered rings the next day. Ginsberg agreed. Fleming (or "Lemming") never picked up the rings. When Rita asked him for them, he distracted her with other matters, including new plans to buy a house in Galway.

Around about this time, to complicate an already complicated triangle, Rita's father heard rumours that John Fleming was married. Not knowing that Rita was now pregnant by the draper's assistant, her father told her not to see him any more. Desperate, Rita confronted John with the ban and the rumour which had provoked it. Fleming first laughed at the story, but agreed to see his girlfriend's worried parent. There was no truth in the rumour, he told Mr Murtagh, who was having second thoughts about the permission he had trustingly extended to Rita to be out all night at "special parties" with Fleming. (Rita may not have confided in her father that on at least two of these occasions, she had slept in Fleming's house in the absence of his "aunt." She would not have known that her presence in the house was explained away to Ellen Fleming's brother as a visit to John Fleming by a "cousin.")

Fleming sadly theorised that the reason for the rumour might be jealousy, although he could not put a name on the rumour-monger. Maybe, he further speculated, people had seen him taking his aunt out for a walk. Over a drink in a pub in Stoneybatter, Fleming became positively collusive with the father.

"We have never been bad friends," he said portentously.

"No, and we never will be if you can prove to me that you're a single man," retorted Murtagh.

Fleming told Murtagh that he had his suspicions. He figured that someone who lived on the same road as he did was spreading the rumours, but he had now worked out a plan to flush out the evil-doer and would be sure of his (or her) name in a day or two.

"I'll go back to the person who said to me that you're a married man," Murtagh offered, "and try to find out where the information came from."

This, Fleming agreed, would be a really great help. He would be back to Murtagh within a couple of days, he promised, and the two men parted on good terms. It was now more than half-way through July, and Rita's condition meant that the time for prevarication was running out.

Ellen's nephew, John Berry, had been away from the Drumcondra residence for a summer holiday, and was coming back on the train, bringing Ellen's sister Rose with him. At 7.20 on the evening of 26 July, the train arrived in Dublin. Ellen did not meet the pair at the station, as they had expected, but there were plenty of taxis at the rank, so they hailed one and set off for the north side of the city. Less than twenty minutes later, Berry and his Aunt Rose were knocking at the front door of the Fleming house. There was no answer, so Berry went next door, remembering the arrangement Ellen Fleming had with the O'Rourkes that they would hold a spare key to her house, in order to allow deliveries if she happened to be away. Berry collected this spare key and let himself and his aunt into the house. When the two of them got to the door leading into the kitchen and the parlour, they found it jammed shut. Exerting some pressure, they overcame the resistance of whatever was holding it closed, getting the door open enough to show them that the obstacle was a dead body. Horror-stricken, they ran next door to the O'Rourkes, who must by now have been having second thoughts about the Flemings as peaceful next-door neighbours of choice. A doctor was called, and quickly arrived, to confirm that the dead person was Ellen Fleming, who had suffered at least twenty blows to the head.

Like a sad parody of the old nursery rhyme about "my son John" who went to bed with his trousers on, "one shoe off and the other shoe on," Ellen had one shoe on and was lying on the other. She was dressed as if she had been getting ready to go out, wearing a little hat which had been perforated by the blows rained upon her. Thrown over a nearby table was her coat, and her gloves rested on the sewing machine. Right beside her lay her purse, containing four pounds in notes, with some silver and copper coins. A window, usually kept open, was closed, and the curtains pulled so that the room was darkened. It seemed that the perpetrator of the appalling crime must have escaped through the scullery door to the back garden.

But it also seemed that the perpetrator had known Ellen Fleming's planned movements for that afternoon, had attacked her without warning and struck her repeatedly and with a concentrated determination to finish her off.

The doctor who had been called to examine Ellen quickly decided that this was undoubtedly murder and that it had happened perhaps two or three hours earlier. He figured that any one of the major injuries, which included incisions on the jaw and a depressed skull-fracture, might have been fatal, and it was also his opinion that Ellen would have bled to death quickly, perhaps within fifteen minutes of the start of the attack. He ordered that the gardaí be summoned.

The gardaí established without much bother that the last time Ellen had been seen alive was around about 4.30 in the afternoon of that summer day. Her husband, John, had been in the garden half an hour earlier than that, trimming the grass with a shears. An insurance agent had arrived in the afternoon and spoken to Ellen and probably also to John.

A search to locate John was now undertaken. Someone had seen him walking along the Bull Wall, the stretch of golden sand backed by dunes which, at that time, was reachable only by a wooden bridge at Clontarf. (There is now a causeway further along the length of the Bull Island.)

About an hour later, John turned up at a friend's house in Clontarf, where he often dropped in on a Wednesday to do bits of gardening. He apologised to the family for being later than usual, saying he had been sunbathing and had stayed too long on the beach. After doing some work in their garden, he joined the family for tea.

Fleming was still in the house of his Clontarf friends when the gardaí descended. They talked to him. Noted suspicious stains on his clothing. Cautioned him. Asked him to accompany them to Mountjoy police station. Told him his wife had been murdered.

"Murder?" he gasped. "Did you say murder? Oh, my God, I will go with you, Sir."

He didn't have much choice about going with them, but it made for a good dramatic moment.

While he was in Mountjoy Station, the gardaí were searching his home and garden, establishing that a claw-hammer was missing. That the Flemings had owned such a hammer was vouched for by Ellen's lodger nephew, John Berry, who not only described it in great detail, but who was able to pick out its mate from a series of those on offer in any hardware store. The one he picked, according to the doctor who had examined the dead woman, was the one most likely to have inflicted the injuries he had seen on the corpse.

Berry did more than discuss claw-hammers. He told the gardaí of the girl who had stayed in the Drumcondra house when his aunt had been away; the girl John Fleming had described as his cousin. The close-woven fabric of lies which was John Fleming's life began to unravel with remarkable speed, providing the gardaí with a motive for the husband to have killed his wife, so that he could marry the girl he had got pregnant and who, together with her family, was becoming more frantic in her demands and her dissatisfaction.

Questioned, John Fleming said virtuously that he knew nothing of the murder. He could know nothing of it, he explained, because he was not at home at the time. The only person he knew was due to be at his home that afternoon was the insurance agent.

If the reference to the insurance agent was an attempt to divert suspicion away from himself, it failed miserably, in view of the examination of Fleming's clothing, which revealed many small human bloodstains. Someone had tried to clean the blood off the clothing. One button, for example, was pristine on its top surface, but had dried blood within the little holes that the thread goes through.

As the gardaí listened to an outpouring of gossip about what now seemed to have been an earlier attempt to murder Ellen Fleming, using poison, they decided they had their man, and Fleming was charged.

On the sidelines, as all this happened, was the twenty-year-old Rita Murtagh. Just as he had promised her father he'd be back to him within a couple of days with a clarification of the rumours about him being married, so Fleming had told Rita he would see her in a couple of days; after he had sorted out the purchase of their dream home in Galway and taken care of a sick relative who needed him badly.

Before he delivered on either of these promises, however, he was personally delivered to prison. On 22 September, before the case came to trial, Rita, still unwed, gave birth to their baby.

John Fleming found himself in court four months after his wife's death. The case, which lasted seven days, riveted newspaper readers. To this day, older Dubliners remember "the Drumcondra murder". A draper's assistant with a mistress was a new concept. Mistresses belonged in medieval history, and murders, whether by poisoning or by claw-hammer, belonged in books by Wilkie Collins or that young Agatha Christie.

Opening the case against Fleming, Senior Counsel M Maguire painted a picture of Ellen Fleming as a dignified and discreet woman making the best of a very bad marital lot, who was not the type to broadcast, even to her closest neighbours, the problems she had with her husband, and whose lips had now been sealed by death. The evidence, Maguire told the jury, would show that his wife was standing in Fleming's way. She was barring the road to a passion which he had developed for another woman.

Within that framework the case proceeded, with all of

those involved in the earlier, putative poisoning incident, called to give evidence. The doctor who had treated the unfortunate Ellen for nerves by recommending a tonic, testified that nobody had tried to get him to come to the Fleming home on the night that John Fleming had purported to make three attempts to get a doctor. Patrick O'Rourke's well-educated guesswork that strychnine had been involved in the incident in 1932 was borne out by evidence that Fleming, in March of that year, had, through a third party, bought ten grains of strychnine which he had claimed he was going to use to poison a troublesome dog.

Because strychnine is a supertoxin, not only would ten grains have taken care of the troublesome dog (about which, significantly, the equable Fleming had never complained to its owner) but it would also have poisoned at least one human. Less than seven drops, or not much more than a taste of strychnine (5mg/kg), is a lethal oral dose.

Mrs O'Rourke, the much put-upon next-door neighbour, testified that Fleming, probably rattled on that March night by his wife's blunt refusal to take any medicinal beverage from him and her claims that he had poisoned the first drink he had given her, had paid a visit next door the following morning to tell the O'Rourkes about a recent purchase of strychnine. He had bought it to poison a dog, he had said, but some of it "might have got loose" in his pocket and got mixed with the chocolate he had then used to make Ellen's hot chocolate drink. Fleming further blurted that he had buried the rest of the strychnine in the lane, and begged Mr and Mrs O'Rourke not to tell his wife about it.

Evidence was also given that the sudden illness of Ellen

Fleming in that month had followed fast on the heels of John Fleming's promise to Rita Murtagh that they'd be able to get married quickly, because his "aunt" had recently suffered a stroke and was likely to move out completely in the near future.

The emotional highpoint of the trial happened on Friday, 17 November, with the arrival in the witness box of Fleming's former girlfriend, Rita Murtagh.

Dramatic Scenes at Dublin Trial

A Witness Faints

Those were the headlines in the following day's *Independent*, over a story that Rita Murtagh, when sworn in, had answered the preliminary questions in a low, level voice, but that as her examination by Mr Maguire, SC proceeded, she had sobbed and seemed on the verge of a complete breakdown.

"Try and be calm, Miss Murtagh," Justice Meredith told her gently. "Everyone has great sympathy for you."

Gathering herself together, Rita told the court about the growing friendship between herself and the accused. However, when asked questions about her belief in his intention to marry her, she came completely adrift, and had to be taken from the court by a probation officer and her own mother. In her absence, her father and mother both testified, as did the jeweller who had taken the order for her engagement and wedding rings. Their evidence was followed by an adjournment, and an attempt to move out of the court those who were just there to gawk. This attempt, made in deference to Rita Murtagh's heightened sensitivities, could not succeed, given that such a court case has to be public and the public are entitled to be present.

Eventually, Rita came back into court, flanked on one

side by the probation officer and on the other by a doctor, and took up a seat behind counsel for the prosecution. In that position, her back was towards the public gallery, and also towards the dock where her former lover sat.

Mr Maguire asked that she be allowed to give evidence from that position, a proposition swiftly and vehemently opposed by Fleming's counsel. The judge said that Rita Murtagh was under the impression that people were staring at her, and this was very trying. Fleming's counsel, unmoved, declared it would be equally trying for him to attempt to cross-examine her in the position she now occupied.

Furthermore, he stated, warming to his theme, if she was allowed to sit there, he would subsequently apply to have every later witness sit in the same place. Faced with this prescription for court chaos, the judge realised he had little choice.

"Try, like a good child," he implored Rita, "if you can come to the witness table."

The girl, who had been weeping silently, head down, during the altercation between the lawyers, now sobbed openly. However, she made the move to the witness table and responded to the questions put to her, telling of her visits to his home, of seeing a woman's fur coat in the house, and of Fleming's explanation that this belonged to his absent aunt. Counsel for Fleming then asked her if she had ever heard, before the summer, any suggestion that Fleming was a married man.

"No," came the quiet reply.

"Was it ever suggested, even as a joke?"

"No."

The barrister continued along these lines and Miss

Murtagh burst into a fit of loud sobbing. The judge said she should be taken out into the air. As she was being assisted from her seat, she fainted, and had to be carried out. Medical testimony was then given that she would be incapable of answering further questions on that day. She did return, briefly, on the following morning, and at the conclusion of her evidence, was verbally head-patted by the judge, who told her (somewhat unrealistically) to go home to her mother and father and forget the court. It had been a very trying time for her, he announced, and she had been a very good girl.

Rita then suffered another swoon, this time into the arms of a garda superintendent, who carried her out of the courtroom "in a fainting condition."

John Fleming's seven hours in the witness box later that Saturday could not have been in sharper contrast to Rita Murtagh's performance. A contemporary report says that "he gave his evidence with great calmness, and emphatically declared that he had nothing whatever to do with the death of his wife." Sitting in the witness chair, in a black overcoat, brown tweed suit, brown shirt and black tie, he must have looked like a trainee Nazi, but his responses to his counsel's queries were serene and deliberate. His counsel did a little advance promotion for him by predicting that the jury would see he was an honest, respectable witness who would tell them a story completely consistent with his innocence.

Fleming outlined his marital and career history, and fairly quickly got to the story of his extra-marital affair. Not that Fleming called it that. He called it "human nature," which seemed to be his personal euphemism for illicit sexual activity.

"Was the subject of marriage discussed between you?" he was asked.

"Yes."

"Was that a serious proposal of yours?"

"No."

His counsel took him through the yarn he had spun for Rita early in the month of his wife's death. No, he admitted, he had never gone to Galway as claimed. No, he had done nothing about purchasing a house in Galway as claimed. No, he was not out of Dublin at all during that time.

So, his counsel asked, what was the purpose of all this flim-flam?

"Putting her off," came the reply.

"Had you any intention of marrying her?"

"No."

So much for *that* . . .

Now it was time to move on to the putative earlier poisoning. Fleming confirmed the purchase of the poison for use on the annoying dog. Asked if he had any intention of poisoning his wife, his response was emphatic – and inhuman.

"None," he said. "She was a breadwinner the same as I was."

His account of the day of the murder included the lawn-trimming in the early afternoon, and then a trip into town to look at the shop windows, followed by a bus ride to Dollymount, where he had gone for a dip around half-past six. Because he had no towel with him, he had then sunbathed for quite a while before making his way to his Clontarf friends' house to help with their gardening and have his evening meal with them.

Cross-examined, Fleming cleverly sought to remove any image the jury might hold of him as a cradle-snatching seducer. Admitting that he had met Rita Murtagh as much as four years prior to the court case, which would have put her, at their first encounter, in her mid-teens, he was quick to paint her as looking much older than she was, and as never telling him her real age. He had assumed, he said virtuously, that she was twenty-one. But, whatever age she was, he had lied to her for three years, and had, he agreed, told Rita just before his wife's murder that she and himself would be married within a fortnight.

Prosecution counsel relentlessly drew attention to the almost incredible scale of untruth which seemed to be Fleming's normal *modus operandi*, recalling the poisoning episode, where he had first claimed to have gone three times for a doctor, but later told the doctor he hadn't gone for him at all. Now, he said he *had* gone for the doctor, despite the same doctor's denial, earlier in the court case, of any such call. Asked to explain why he had told his grievously ill wife that the doctor would be with her at any moment, when he knew the doctor would never appear, he was ostentatiously reasonable about the whole thing.

"I had to give a reply to my wife," he explained. "I had to say something."

"And you said something which was untrue?"

"When I came back, I had to pretend to my wife that he was coming."

It was at this point that Fleming's lies began to be mutually incompatible. Asked why he had told the doctor the following day that his wife had been suffering from nerves, he said that it was because his wife had looked for the doctor's services "from pretence." But then he said that he thought a stroke and nerves were the same thing, and maybe his wife had a stroke, because, as he admitted, "she was in agony."

"Why didn't you get in a doctor, then?" demanded the prosecuting attorney.

Because, Fleming said implausibly, his wife would only have her normal doctor, and so he had concentrated his efforts on getting that doctor.

When it got to the question of the bloodstains on his clothing the day of the murder, Fleming claimed that he had cut his hand the day before, and had worn the same shirt.

The draper's assistant told the court that he always wore the one shirt for a full week. He did not explain, and obviously could not explain, why his clothing had been found by the State Pathologist to have been spattered with more than fifty droplets of blood – a spattering quite consistent with the attack on his wife, where the rise and fall of the weapon from the bloody headwounds would have spread a multiplicity of blood droplets, but not at all consistent with a minor cut to his hand. Much was made of his "alibi," but the jury may have thought less, rather than more, of him as a result of his attempt to line up the insurance agent who was making his routine visit to the house, as a possible suspect.

They quickly found him guilty, and the judge, assuming the black cap, sentenced him to death. An appeal was lodged, on the basis that evidence of a previous alleged murder attempt should not have been heard by the jury during the trial. The tripartite Court of Criminal Appeal dismissed this, viewing the earlier attempt as so inextricably mixed up with the relations between him and his wife that it could not be excluded from the consideration of the jury. The court complimented Fleming's counsel on having argued his case with conspicuous ability. The same counsel promptly sought to appeal against this latest judgement, but the Court denied him the right to appeal, and execution was fixed for 5 January 1934. In the weeks between the appeal and execution date, a petition was presented, seeking mercy for Fleming, to the Minister for Justice, who declined to act upon it.

Fleming was duly hanged by Pierrepoint in Mountjoy Prison on the appointed date. Albert Pierrepoint had become an executioner in 1931 and was Britain's official executioner from the thirties until 1956. Because he succeeded his father, the name Pierrepoint was a constant on the short Home Office list of qualified executioners for Great Britain and Ireland. Albert Pierrepoint, a discreet and dignified man whose "day job" was running his own pub, carried out in excess of one hundred executions, more than any other executioner on record.

The executioner in Shaw's *Saint Joan* speaks of his job as "a hugely skilled mystery." Albert Pierrepoint would have agreed. He was initiated into some of that mystery by his father, then undertook an official hangman's course, and finally accompanied his uncle (also an executioner – it was something of a family speciality) as his assistant, using every execution as a tutorial.

In the little room in the prison where we were to pass the night, (my uncle) would explain to me his summing-up of the prisoner, the kind of man he was and the drop he was going to give him: why he was going to ignore the Home Office table and give perhaps a nine-inch longer drop because of what he had observed; what snags he anticipated, if any, and how he intended to deal with him. I would listen to him and absorb his experience, and know that he was really passing on to me my father's store of knowledge and the fruits of that experience, because it had been my father who had taught him. (Albert Pierrepoint, *Pierrepoint: Executioner*, London 1974.)

Fleming was lucky to be hanged by Albert Pierrepoint, because Pierrepoint's claim, all his professional life, was that he had never put a criminal through the horrors often experienced at the hands of earlier hangmen. He had perfected a method he described as "quick, certain and humane." Not all executions by the rope could be so described. Many of today's prison officers tell stories they heard from an earlier generation, of hangings in Mountjoy where the officers had to drag on the legs of the man being executed, to speed his strangling. A properly placed hangman's knot means that the criminal dies virtually instantaneously of a dislocated neck, not by decapitation or strangling.

Criminals awaiting the hangman's noose lived – and sometimes brought about their own deaths – in the horrors of anticipation of a botched execution. After Hermann Goering's suicide, the Reichsmarshal's chaplain was quoted as saying that he had taken his own life rather than face the possibility of hanging, and suffocating, for perhaps a quarter of an hour.

"I have hanged several people myself," he told the chaplain before taking poison, "and I know how it is done. The hangman will make the knot somewhat loose and I shall be slowly strangled."

Goering may have been right. Field Marshal Keitel, convicted along with Goering at the Nuremberg Trials, was said to have lived a horrific twenty minutes on the rope when he was executed.

Pierrepoint, who often came to Ireland to carry out executions, went about the task of giving Fleming a speedy and dignified death on that bitterly cold January morning. In spite of the cold, a crowd of several hundred people, many of them women, gathered outside an hour before the hanging was due to happen.

As eight o'clock struck, a section of the crowd began to say the Rosary, some of the older women breaking into tears. Not long afterwards, the gate of Mountjoy swung open and a warder emerged to post the notice that John Fleming had paid the full penalty for the murder of his wife.

"Leave Your Estate to Me and I'll Look After Your Wife"

The Northern Ireland Doctor who Got Away with Mass Murder

If you were the casting director for a modern soap opera, and you were seeking an actor to play the local doctor, you'd never pick John Bodkin Adams. For one thing, even if you put him in modern clothes, he would still look irretrievably Edwardian. For another, he would not match current stereotypes of the GP. Small (5'5"), grossly overweight (estimated at eighteen stone), he had little in the way of hair and was over-endowed in the jowl department.

But the quietly spoken tubby doctor with the Northern accent literally enslaved many of his patients, particularly those who were female and advanced in years, and the odds are that, over several decades, he not only enslaved them, but murdered them in large numbers. And got away with it.

Dr John Bodkin Adams was born in 1899 in Northern Ireland and went to medical school there, but shortly after graduation went to Eastbourne, where, within a matter of a few years, he was the doctor of choice. Not that he did extraordinary ground-breaking research. Not that he had innovative therapies for his patients.

Two things made Dr Bodkin Adams a favourite medic in Eastbourne. One was his bedside manner. He was never in a hurry, never impatient. He always found the time to charm elderly women patients, patting their hands and stroking their hair. The other factor in his favour was that he had a liberal hand when it came to issuing prescriptions for morphine. In an area where older people came to live out their retirement, he had a constant supply of vulnerable, and often wealthy, old people who could speedily be addicted to morphine or heroin, and who might be influenced to alter their wills in his favour.

Once the change was made to the will, the patient became considerably more vulnerable, and a slightly larger dose might depress breathing and give them a peaceful, if unsought and murderous, end.

Bodkin Adams practised for more than three decades in the same town, growing richer with every passing year, as patient after patient (more than 130 in all) left him the bulk of their property in their wills. It is estimated that these bequests, in financial terms alone, would now be worth several million pounds, and, in addition to the cash, he inherited jewellery, antique furniture and cars, including a few Rolls-Royces.

Not everybody was happy with the doctor from the wee North. Alice Whitton's niece was seriously unhappy when Alice died in 1936 and left her doctor £3,000, which was, at the time, a very substantial amount. The niece went to court to contest the will, but lost. As well as the occasional court case, there was gossip. But the doctor's popularity and wealth grew without any major interruption during the war and in the years thereafter.

It was not until the mid-fifties that the British police became seriously concerned. Long before the days when computers would do correlations and draw the attention of the authorities to therapeutic or other judgements of a doctor which seemed out of kilter with the mainstream of medical practice, it was noted that quite an extraordinary number of Dr Bodkin Adams's patients seem to die of two ailments. Almost 70 per cent of them, according to his death certificates, died either from cerebral thrombosis or cerebral haemorrhage. That wasn't likely. In fact, it wasn't possible. Or else Eastbourne needed serious study as a locus for a unique pattern of illness.

Suspicion of Dr John Bodkin Adams was beginning to grow. The successor to Alice Whitton's niece was William Mawhood's wife. Mrs Mawhood was named Esther, and her husband had been a friend of Dr Bodkin Adams for a long, long time. In fact, William had lent him a few thousand pounds to buy his first house – at a time when a few thousand pounds was all it took to buy a house outright. In 1956, William was wealthy. William was dying. And Dr Bodkin Adams was on the make. "Leave your estate to me and I'll look after your wife," he told William, having first asked Edith to leave the room. Leave the room she did, but not move out of earshot, and when she heard the doctor make his proposition to her husband, she was livid. "I grabbed my gold-headed walking stick and struck out at the doctor and chased him around the bed," she later recalled. "He ran out of the room and as he dashed down the stairs I threw my stick at him."

Perhaps because Mrs Mawhood had little practice at aiming gold-headed walking sticks at fat little fleeing doctors, she missed, pranging one of her own vases. As Bodkin Adams made it out the front door, she yelled at him never to come back.

Another family, which had a tradition for generations of dividing the estate of parents equally among the surviving children, found that the doctor had persuaded their mother to change her will before she died, leaving the bulk of the family estate to him.

The doctor was without shame. As time went on, it seemed as if he was without judgement, either. When a comatose patient signs a will making his doctor the beneficiary with an X, it is understandable if family and police become a little edgy.

When more and more patients, without ever mentioning their intentions to their families, are found to have, shortly before death (of cerebral haemorrhage) *doubly* changed their wills, not only to benefit Dr John Bodkin Adams, but also to request cremation, relatives and the forces of law and order are likely to become seriously concerned.

The serious concern, after many years, resulted in the exhuming of two bodies. Hilda and Clara Neil-Miller had both been patients of Dr Bodkin Adams. Elderly sisters, one (Hilda) died just a little over a year before the second. Hilda left all of her money to Clara. Clara left all of her money to Bodkin Adams. Clara's death certificate said she had succumbed to coronary thrombosis. Her exhumed body said different. It testified to a death from pneumonia. But if she had died of something as simple as pneumonia – so often and so peacefully fatal in the early years of the century that it was known as the "old man's friend" – it seemed puzzling that the doctor should have gone out of his way to distract anybody investigating her death from the realisation that she had died of pneumonia. Until investigators came upon evidence which convinced them that the doctor had quite deliberately sought to give poor old Clara the illness that killed her.

Clara had lived in an old people's home. One of the other residents had noted that the doctor had spent almost an hour with his patient one winter night, before leaving with the comment that she was suffering from influenza. After he had gone, the resident decided to pop her head into Clara's room and see how she was doing. She was horrified by what she saw. All of the bed coverings had been pulled off Clara and thrown over the rail at the end of the bed. The old woman's nightdress had been rolled right up to her neck. Every window in the room was open, on a bitterly cold night. Small wonder the influenza ripened into full-scale pneumonia.

Small wonder the doctor, signing the death certificate, would wish to suggest that something unrelated to exposure had killed the poor woman.

Having exhumed Clara some three years later, the police were unsurprised to find that the doctor had done very well financially as a result of her death. They were a bit more surprised to find that he had done well financially before she ever passed away. Cheques had been made out for sums like £300 and £500 – the equivalent of many thousand pounds today. The police were baffled as to why an elderly patient, while still alive, would have been making cheques of this size out to her doctor, especially since all that ailed her, before the pneumonia, was flu.

Every finding the police made led to another finding. Not only was the doctor profiting from the deaths of the residents in the old people's home, he was profiting from their survival as well, since he had a financial interest in the place. The woman who ran it knew where the bodies were buried, what the doctor had really done, and how he had benefited down through the years. The police talked to her. Very gently. Very persistently. Sure that they had not frightened her off, they moved in for one last major interview, only to find that she had died on one of the intervening days and had been expeditiously cremated on the doctor's instructions. "I always had a feeling, but no positive clue, that Adams speeded her on the way," commented Scotland Yard Chief Superintendent Charles Hewett, who was in charge of the case. "It was too much of a coincidence."

Coincidence followed coincidence. Patient followed patient into the grave – or the crematorium. It was like a prayer before dying. You changed your will to make Adams a major beneficiary, you added a codicil to make sure you'd be cremated after death, and then you snuffed it within a matter of weeks.

Adams had an effrontery which, in retrospect, is astonishing. One man was helped to change his will when heavily drugged and died within a week or so, although the presenting illness that had brought him into Dr Adams's care was a broken ankle. Some of his patients were so openly addicted to the injections he gave them that their families were embarrassed by their desperation as a "fix" came due. Some of the nurses working with his patients were in no doubt that he was a lethal practitioner, and were courageous enough to say so. One state registered nurse watched him arrive to look after an elderly widow, and heard him announce that he was going to give Mrs Kilgour an injection to give her a good night's sleep. The nurse watched as the doctor drew the liquid drug into the syringe – and kept drawing more liquid into it until she knew he had exceeded any normal dose. "This will keep her quiet," he said, and left.

The nurse was left with a comatose patient who did not survive twenty-four hours. By the time Dr Adams was due to visit again, the nurse was waiting for him. "Mrs Kilgour is dead," she told him, getting straight to the point. "You realise, doctor, that you have killed her?"

The same nurse then went to the police with her information. In the meantime, the death certificate issued, certifying the cause of death as cerebral haemorrhage, and the will was probated, giving Adams money and an antique clock.

Now and again, there was the one that got away. Mrs Pilling got away. The heiress to a Lancashire cotton-milling fortune, she had the flu. Now, even in the fifties, a reasonably robust older patient could expect to recover quickly from flu under the care of a good GP. Factor Dr John Bodkin Adams into the equation, however, and the prognosis deteriorated. Two weeks after his first visit, Mrs Pilling was verging on coma. "At first, we thought she was dying of cancer and that the doctor was being kind by not telling us," her daughter remembered, explaining what happened when the family took their "dying" mother back home for her final days. Two weeks after they took her home, the coma had retreated, the flu was cured and Mrs Pilling wanted to go to the races. "Had I not taken her away, I am quite satisfied she would have died," concluded the daughter.

Mrs Pilling started with minor illness and very nearly died. Mrs Hullett started with no illness at all, and did die.

It was her story which finally called a halt to the inexorable progress of the murderous medical juggernaut.

As in so many other cases, Mrs Hullett and her husband Jack were friends of Dr Adams. Friends and patients. When, in 1955, Jack sickened, he mentioned to several nurses that he was fortunate to have such a good doctor. In due course, helped by a dose of morphia (strange treatment, given that what was wrong with him was a heart condition), Jack Hullett died. His wife inherited the bulk of his estate, although he had remembered to take care of Dr Adams to the tune of £500. Jack Hullett might have saved his wife's life if he had reversed the bequests. From the moment of Jack's death, Dr Adams was a constant presence in his widow's life, prescribing heavy doses of narcotic to help her sleep.

People working for the Hulletts had reservations when they noted that, several weeks after Jack's demise, his widow was still staggering around during the day as if she were drunk. Two friends, a husband and wife, invited her to stay with them, in the hope of weaning her from the medication. "But she rushed back after twenty-four hours to get to her pills again," shrugged the friends. "We saw her disintegrating mentally through them. We saw her turning into a drug addict."

They did not see her die, but die she did, precisely four months after her husband, having conveniently made out a cheque for a thousand pounds to Dr Adams a day or two beforehand.

There was an inquest, and at that inquest, the coroner didn't sugar-coat his words. He thought Adams's approach to his patient appalling, in its lack of second opinion, its lack of proper daily medical supervision, and its eventual diagnosis of cerebral haemorrhage.

"I honestly did what I thought was best for her," was Adams's response to all of this.

"There has been an extraordinary degree of careless treatment," the coroner said disgustedly.

At this point – no sooner, despite a recurring pattern of profit-by-death lasting three decades – Scotland Yard was called in. Much investigation was done, and it was decided that Adams should be charged with murder. One murder; that of a widow in her seventies named Edith Morell. The Morell case, to the prosecution lawyers, looked like a cert. "It was such a clear and obvious case of murder that I should have thought no jury could have regarded it in any other way," was how one of the legal men put it.

When he was convicted, the legal team decided, he could then be charged with further murders. Scotland Yard were morally certain that Adams had killed about twenty-five of his patients.

Except that he was not convicted of the Morell charge.

The case was lost because the defence lawyer, although he had no love for his fat little client, still had a sense of strategy. Queen's Counsel Geoffrey Lawrence planned his case knowing that if Dr John Bodkin Adams went into the witness box in his own defence, he would be sliced to ribbons by the splendid cross-examination of Attorney General Sir Reginald Manningham-Buller. So Lawrence decided not to put Adams in the witness box at all, robbing Manningham-Buller of the opportunity for effective grandstanding.

But the case was also lost because the Attorney General's confidence greatly outweighed his judgement. Hewett, the Scotland Yard detective who had pieced together an encyclopaedia-sized portfolio of evidence against the doctor, was bitter about this. "Adams was allowed to escape because the law made an ass of itself," he shrugged. "I will never forget that conference we had with Manningham-Buller in the Attorney General's office at the House of Commons . . . I felt sick with disbelief when he announced he was going for Mrs Morrell. It was madness when we had so many better cases with more specific evidence – and, what's more important, with bodies."

Because Edith Morell had been cremated, the best forensic scientist of the day, Dr Francis Camps, could be no part of the prosecution team. Had a patient been chosen whose body could be – or had been – exhumed, then Camps, whose appearances in court were always a *tour de force*, would have been a huge asset to the prosecutors. As it was, they had to do without him completely. But the Attorney General was unworried by this, ebullient in his belief that he would wipe out Adams on cross-examination, and never giving countenance to the possibility that Adams would not subject himself to that process.

Six years after Mrs Morrell's death, in 1957, a jury at the Old Bailey heard that during the month and a half leading up to her death, Adams had prescribed heroin and barbiturates for her in amounts that would choke a horse. On the day of her death, he injected more than seventeen grains of morphine into her. The maximum recommended dose at the time was a quarter-grain. But his counsel confused some of the nurses by producing their notebooks of the time. Some of their six-year-old recollections did not quite match, in every detail, what the notebooks revealed, and a reasonable doubt was instilled into the minds of jurors. Without Adams in the witness box to be hounded about his practices and his gains, the case was a wash-out, and after less than an hour's absence, the jury found him not guilty. The knock-on effect of this was to convince the Director of Public Prosecutions that no *other* case would stick against Adams, and so all the evidence, all the exhumations, all the anger of relatives and police, went for naught.

It led to small mitigation of that anger when a few months after the murder trial, Adams was found guilty of failing to keep a record of dangerous drugs and of forging National Health Service prescriptions, and a few months later again was struck off by the General Medical Council. Not that the striking-off lasted long.

In the early sixties, he was re-admitted and allowed to work as a doctor again, with the restriction that he could not prescribe dangerous drugs. Enough patients came back to guarantee him a comfortable living. Enough of them left him monies in their will to make that living more than comfortable, and when he retired, he had hundreds of thousands of pounds-worth of investments to live on.

At that point, in his sixties, he might have returned to Northern Ireland, where scandal was unlikely to follow him, but he chose to stay put, dying in his eighties in Sussex in 1983, remembered bitterly by surviving relatives and by detectives as possibly the most blatantly successful mass murderer in modern times.

MATRICIDE AND A GRIM NIGHT ON LOVER'S LANE

A Remarkable Conviction without a Corpse

When you see a small car parked in among others in a well-known lover's lane in suburbia, and when you – dimly, because of the winter evening darkness – see one of the figures within that car embracing the other, shorter figure, it might be fair to infer that here is a boyfriend cuddling his girlfriend.

On the night of 17 February 1936, however, the taller figure in the Baby Austin with the sun-roof, parked in Corbawn Lane in Shankill on Dublin's southside, was not a boyfriend embracing his girl. It was a son embracing his mother. And she was dead.

But let's backtrack a bit.

First, there was Dr Ball. Dr Preston Ball, an eminent medical man, specialising in nervous disorders, whose rooms were in Baggot Street. Dr Ball had married his wife Vera (aka Lavinia) just after the turn of the century, and the couple had two sons. The first-born arrived two years after their marriage, while the second did not arrive until 1916, twelve years later.

Happy the marriage was not, and that was putting it mildly. Never mind how it had come about (and there were later references to puerperal depression as having afflicted Vera Ball after the birth of Edward, the second son), Vera was a highly strung woman who had, over the years, developed a spectacular and very active loathing for her husband. This manifested itself in her insulting him in front of patients, to whom she described him as a useless doctor, while recommending that they favour some other physician with their business. She also persuaded people to ring him so that he had to make trips out to the country to see patients who turned out not to exist. Eleven years after Edward was born, the couple separated, Mrs Ball living in Booterstown while her husband resided on Pembroke Road.

The eldest son had departed the dysfunctional home earlier on to study veterinary science in England.

The problems continued, however. Vera Ball was well off, and had a part-time job with the Hospitals Sweepstakes, not to mention annuities which made her financial situation very comfortable. That didn't stop her stealing. Not only was she a kleptomaniac, but her own (woman) doctor had seen her on several occasions taking money from the doctor's own handbag. She was extremely excitable, but also given to long depressions characterised by a refusal to talk to anybody.

Nor was Edward a ray of sunshine. When he was only sixteen, his father, who evidently was concerned as to his sanity, took him to Harley Street for examination by a British specialist, who interviewed the young man and noted that, while he was of average IQ, he wasn't high on moral responsibility or common sense, and had a tendency to talk happily about suicide. The specialist felt that a holiday with his father, followed by a spell in a school which was heavy on the discipline, would get Edward nicely shaped up. His father was less optimistic, believing that Edward, who proceeded to fail all his school exams and exhibited no ambition whatever, should probably be locked up for his own good. This option was passionately opposed by Vera.

Instead of incarceration in one of the mental hospitals or asylums of the time, Edward was sent off to school in Shrewsbury, leaving in 1934 with a less than impressive academic record. The young man moved to London, where he worked in a bank and studied drama. Around this time, he did seem to have two ambitions, neither held very strongly. One was to drive a train. The other was to act. However, he moved to Paris the following year with the objective of training for a diplomatic career.

When he left France, which was not long after his arrival, he travelled with a police escort to the port of departure. This courtesy was extended because of his exercise of perhaps inherited skills (he had stolen money from his landlady) and his creativity, as evidenced by his forging of a passport.

Home came Edward, patently troubled and in trouble, to spend time with his father, and, when that failed to work out, to spend time with his equally troubled mother. For a while, he managed to exist in rented rooms, but was regarded as a queerly moody individual who more than once threatened to commit suicide using alcohol and aspirin. Like his mother, Edward veered wildly between elation and depression.

Put a combination like that of the Ball mother and son into a house and the end result is predictable. Wild screaming matches happened frequently between mother and son.

On the night of 17 February 1936, Mrs Ball's Baby Austin, complete with sun-roof, was parked in a cul-de-sac near the sea at Shankill from about a quarter to ten onwards. In the morning it was still there, arousing the curiosity of a man delivering newspapers. Except that now, it was not neatly parked. It was jammed up against a barrier which had been erected to prevent motorists accidentally driving into the sea, the driver's door and the sun-roof were both wide open and there was bloodstaining on the upholstery. In addition, there was a bloodstained towel and some equally saturated blotting-paper on the back seat.

The newspaper seller told the gardaí, who came to examine the car, which also showed bloodstains on its wheels. There was more blood on the ground beside the vehicle, which they were able to identify, from paperwork in the glove compartment, as belonging to Mrs Lavinia Ball, resident at St Helen's Road, Booterstown. The gardaí speedily repaired to this address.

It was a stylish semi-detached house near what is now the Blackrock Clinic, and was, according to reports at the time, furnished "sumptuously and elegantly."

When the policemen arrived, they were greeted by Vera Ball's maid, who was organising things for the lunch Mrs Ball was planning to host for two friends on that day. The maid said that Edward had gone out earlier, carrying a suitcase, and that when she had knocked on the door of Mrs Ball's bedroom, she had got no response. She might have been more worried about this lack of response, were it not for a puzzling distraction: the fact that the first thing she had noticed on her arrival at her employer's house that morning was that the stairs, the kitchen and the hallway were sodden with water. Edward had made no reference to this evidence of inundation, merely expressed the wish that the ladies might have an enjoyable lunch.

They didn't. One of them, the host, was missing, her bedroom door locked. The gardaí called for high-level support, and returned in the late afternoon accompanied by a superintendent. Edward then arrived home, all cool and collected and willing to answer questions about his mother and her whereabouts. She had, he stated, gone off the previous night to stay with a female friend, but hadn't returned. Edward had, at this time, already talked to his father, who was aware of the finding of the car in Corbawn Lane. He went further, in his efforts to be helpful, listing in great detail the clothing his mother had worn the previous evening when she departed the house.

No key to Vera Ball's bedroom was forthcoming, so strong garda shoulders were applied with vigour to the door.

When it gave, and the gardaí moved carefully inside, they were hit by a wave of hot air coming from an electric fire within the sealed room, which seemed to have been directed towards drying a stain on the carpet. The gardaí asked the maid to have a look at Mrs Ball's wardrobe, and she was able to tell them that the clothes Edward had described his mother as wearing when she left the house were all present, correct – and hanging in the wardrobe.

Edward's father came around to the house to offer any help he could to the gardaí, and was doorstepped by journalists, to whom he revealed some details of Mrs Ball's erratic mental health, including a mention of a nervous breakdown and of her being hospitalised for it. Dr Ball, according to the reporters, "did not incline to the view that Mrs Ball was the victim of foul play."

Dr Ball might not incline in that direction, but the gardaí now decided that, with or without a body, the murder of Mrs Ball should be taken as a "given," and they were publicly stating that belief four days after the murder. They were certain that it was murder, and they were certain it had happened in her home, where they had found a hatchet, of which more later. Pushed, gardaí who were members of the investigating team even conveyed to journalists their belief that the woman had been murdered in her bed.

Their investigations followed two distinct lines. One was of the areas outside the house where there was a possibility that the body might turn up. The other was the continued interviewing of Edward Ball.

The external search was massive, involving everything from digging up dumps to surveying the land from aircraft. The dump at Booterstown, receiving-post at that time for rubbish from all houses in the area, including that of Vera Ball, was combed by gardaí, who did extensive digging at the site. On Thursday, two planes from Irish Air Ferries spent four hours in the air, flying along the coast from Howth Head to Bray. The following day, it was planned, based on what had been spotted on Thursday, that the planes would concentrate on Shankill Bay, flying at a low altitude. In spite of the growing garda conviction that the dead woman had probably been heaved into the sea not 200 yards from where her abandoned Austin car had been found, investigation also went on at the abandoned Ballycorus mine tunnel in the Dublin mountains on the off-chance that the corpse had been dumped there. Other gardaí could be seen with grappling hooks, searching the stretch of coast along Vico Road. Boats went out in the sea around Dalkey, as gardaí tried to establish the object that was attracting the attention of considerable numbers of seabirds there, and land-based gardaí were putting heavy objects into the sea from various angles, near Corbawn Lane, in order to determine which direction the currents took in the area. There was little reason to be optimistic, as one observer stated, since in the case of four drownings around the Dun Laoghaire area in the previous few years, only one body was found, and that one was washed up on the Isle of Skye off the Scottish coast.

Corbawn Lane, meanwhile, had become something of a pilgrimage site, with visitors coming to have a look at the place where the Austin Seven had been found. With only two light-poles throwing light on the first few yards, and the rest of the area shadowed by trees, it was a forbidding and threatening cul-de-sac.

On Friday afternoon, however, interest suddenly shifted back to the house on St Helen's Road, for the very simple reason that Edward Ball had plunged out of a second-storey bathroom window and landed in the grounds of the house with a considerable thump. Two gardaí who were guarding the house rushed to the back garden and found the nineteen-year-old lying on the ground directly under the toilet window. He had not been interrogated directly beforehand. Now the gardaí called both a doctor and his father. The doctor (wrongly, as it later turned out) decided that his injuries were minor and required no hospital treatment. Young Edward was tucked into bed, and afternoon drew into evening.

At seven o'clock, the front door of the house was quickly opened, and Edward Ball was escorted out, leaning heavily on the arms of two plainclothes gardaí, with a third officer awkwardly supporting him from behind. He wore a black overcoat and a grey trilby, and looked both pale and wan. The gardaí between them loaded him into a waiting car and drove off, taking Edward to the Bridewell, where he was formally charged with matricide. "I do not feel like saying anything at the moment," was the accused man's only response to the charge.

From the Bridewell, Ball was taken to hospital, where he was found to have sustained rather more than abrasions in the fall from the bathroom window. He had a fracture of the neck and a broken arm, which were then treated in the Richmond Hospital, where he stayed until just before the court case started. At that point he was transferred to Mountjoy Prison.

Mrs Ball's body was never found. But gardaí certainty that she was dead was reinforced by a statement they had taken from her son two days after the murder, although they did not make this statement public. According to Edward, he had gone to see his mother five days before the murder. The reason for his visit was to tell her he could no longer manage the finances of living in a flat and needed to live with her. Her enthusiasm for this proposition was non-existent, but she reluctantly agreed. It was an agreement she continually revised, however, driving her son wild in the process. "She did not want me to stay with her," he recalled. "She wanted me either to stay with my father or to take rooms in town. I told her my father would not have me and that I could not afford rooms . . ."

By the night of the murder, he claimed, Vera Ball was "fussed" about a lot more than the presence of her son in the house. She was planning a lunch, some cigarettes had gone missing, and she had a row with the maid, the end-result of which was the firing of the maid. (It is not possible to establish if the maid who turned up for work the following day is the same one who received her cards on Sunday night.)

Having fired the maid, Mrs Ball, according to her son, then moved on to a stream of consciousness covering almost every unsatisfactory facet of her life, which, *in toto*, she described as a failure. Her marriage had gone bad although she had tried to make it work. Her older son wasn't amounting to anything, although she had done her best for him. Her younger son was also destined for failure, although she had done everything she could think of for him, too. The fact that he had managed to break a cup during the meal surfaced in this litany of rage, too.

"She said that life was hopeless and that she wished she were dead," her son recalled.

He claimed to have tried to calm her down. Given their matched capacity for manic moods, this would have been the counselling equivalent of the blind leading the blind. "I want you to promise me something," he claimed she suddenly said to him. "I want you to promise me that you will do all you can to prevent people thinking I am a coward."

When saying this, he described her as "extremely distraught and weeping copiously." He nevertheless thought little of it. Mrs Ball went upstairs and didn't come back down. After more than an hour, Edward said, he had gone up to find out why she wasn't coming down, and found his mother lying on her bed with blood streaming from her neck. The source of the wound, he claimed, was a double-edged Gillette razor blade.

He claimed to have thought of calling for help, but never did so, remembering her last words. "I then worked like a machine," he said. "Very rapidly. Not being able to hide her in the small house, I decided to put her in the car. I took her underneath the arms and pulled her out of bed, at which she fell on the floor and a lot of blood spilled."

Putting her arms over his shoulders, he lifted her legs so that her head and the upper part of her body were on his shoulder. At the car, he rested her legs on the ground and opened the passenger door of the car, sliding her inside. The next problem was driving, which he had not done for four years. Although he could get the engine started, he couldn't recollect how to reverse the Austin, and ended up pushing it out on to the road.

In the process, he walloped the car off the gatepost. When he got moving, he forgot to put on the lights, and was lucky he didn't get himself stopped by a guard on the road for driving without lights. Along Sydney Parade he drove, up Ailesbury Road and on to the Stillorgan Road.

Edward's recollections of Corbawn Lane did not include the relatively new barrier preventing a driver from going straight into the sea, which seems to have been his first intention. Balked, he got out of the car and walked down to the sea. While there were other parked cars there, he held his mother as if hugging her, and nobody bothered him. Once the other cars were gone, he decided to try to get around the barrier in order to drive the car into the sea. The car wasn't as small as he thought, however, and it got stuck. "Then I took my mother out of the car and pulled her down the roadway leading to the sea," he told the gardaí.

Not only did he heave his dead mother into the sea, but he wrapped up the razor blade with which he said she had taken her life, and dropped it, too, into the sea.

Mother disposed of, Edward now faced the fact that he was not going to be able to move the car. Keeping his wits about him to some extent, he opened the door and the sun-roof in order to get the smell of blood out of the vehicle. Nevertheless, since he forgot to remove the bloodstained blotting paper and towel from the rear seat, it was something of a pointless exercise. Moving away from Corbawn Lane, he hitched a lift back to his own neighbourhood and reached his own home in the early hours of the morning, where he set to work, frantically, to clean up, using a tablecloth in what appears to have been an irrational desire not to use up all the dishtowels in the kitchen, and putting the electric fire on to dry up the bedroom carpet.

All bedclothes and other loose items which had trapped blood were bundled into a suitcase, which he put aside, to be disposed of later. Not all of the bloodied cloth found its way into the suitcase. The gardaí, even before they had broken down the door of his mother's bedroom, had, unbeknownst to Edward, already found a bundle of bloodstained linen wrapped up in wet newspaper in his own room. This bundle he may have forgotten in his wild frenzy of nightmare spring cleaning, which also included making up his mother's bed afresh and then moving to the kitchen, where one of the grisly tasks he undertook was to throw blood clots out into the back garden. As dawn came, he went to bed, briefly. Then it was time to get up, get out and get rid of the suitcase, which he left with the wife of a friend of his.

Although Edward Ball managed to get rid of his mother's body, which has never been found, he left so many other clues inside and outside the house that he might have been better off if he had never embarked on the business of concealment in the first place.

When the matricide case opened on 18 May 1936, the court was so overcrowded that four gardaí in uniform and counsel, in wig and gown, were forced to take seats in the dock. The prosecution pointed out that Edward was the only person with the means, the motive and the opportunity to murder Mrs Ball.

Evidence came from servants who worked in the Ball house of fights, rows, reconciliations, threats and emotional roller-coastering between mother and son. Contrariwise, one of Mrs Ball's friends, a member of the Society of Friends who refused to take the oath and whose husband, attempting to explain the refusal, very nearly found himself in contempt of court, interpreted the relationship as one of almost total peace.

A garda produced two letters which had been found in Edward Ball's pockets after the fall from the bathroom window, and these were read aloud in court, as the accused man wept bitterly.

The first was addressed to the coroner, and asked him to ensure that Ball's golf clubs were given to a friend after his death. The second was to his father, and read as follows:

My dear Dad

I want to thank you very much for sending me supplies of food. I shall never see you again, and before I take my life, I wish to say how very sorry I am for all the trouble I have caused you. I haven't been a good son, and although you have been a very good father in some ways, I will say if you had not been so hard on me a great deal of trouble would have been avoided.

I have always loved my mother more than you, because I am certain she loves me, but please know that I love you tenderly . . . Things in the past few days have been unbearable, and I claim the right to take my own life.

Your ever-loving son, Edward

Edward's claim that his mother had taken her own life with a razor blade, which was contradicted in neither of these "suicide" notes, was made short shrift of by technical testimony, which left the court in no doubt that a hatchet found in the house with human blood on it had been the instrument of her death. Nor was it helped by the fact that only about a whiskey-glassful of blood was found in the bed, whereas a severed artery would have spilled six or seven pints into the bed and bedclothes. Anyway, medical witnesses opined, so decisive and deep a stroke with a double-sided razor in the neck area would be unusual, at the least.

Summing up, the judge told the jury that three verdicts were open to them:

1. Guilty of murder with malice aforethought;
2. Guilty but insane;
3. Acquittal.

"The outstanding peculiarity of this case," he told them, "is that the body was never found. There is a popular idea that no prosecution is possible for murder when the body is not found. As you have observed during the case, the law is that where the body has not been found it is still open to the state to succeed in a prosecution for murder with malice aforethought, but there must be established three issues. The State must prove that the person alleged to have been murdered is dead, that the person met his or her death with violence, and that the violence was the felonious act with malice aforethought of the person accused. In this case," added the judge significantly, "the difficulty is upon the third ground."

While the judge had left the jury in no doubt that it was legally possible to try someone for murder without having a body to demonstrate that death had actually happened, their task was not made easier by the absence of Mrs Ball's corpse. As GK Chesterton once said, "The body is the chief witness in every murder," and without the body, the jury had to concentrate on inanimate objects which might have been used on the missing body. Consequently, during their five-hour consideration of the evidence, the jury asked for the recall of the maid, in order to find out if Mrs Ball had owned double-sided razorblades. Answering the foreman's question, the maid said that she had never known Mrs Ball to have or use a safety-razor. The jury then retired again and an hour-and-a-half later returned with their verdict: guilty but insane.

The verdict was seen as a surprise, in view both of the defence contention that the accused suffered from dementia praecox (see page 23) and of the summing-up of the judge, which was sympathetic to the defendant. Ball was sent to Dundrum Criminal Lunatic Asylum, from which he was released after the war. At that point, he went to England to work with the Automobile Association. He later moved to Australia, where he died at the beginning of the 1990s.

"In the Name of God, What Happened to Him . . . ?"

A Double Murder in Wicklow

It was typical of Margaret Nolan that she was at a meeting of the Irish Farmers' Association that night. Margaret, aged sixty, had taken over the running of the family farm of 170 acres when her husband Paddy died ten years earlier, and had won the admiration of neighbours for the professionalism with which she operated it. Margaret had the help of her twenty-four-year-old daughter, Ann.

Margaret Nolan was a lot more than an efficient farmer. She was a warm, kind woman, who, conscious of how lonely rural Ireland can be, had, not long beforehand, suggested to a local widow in her eighties that if the older woman were ever afraid at night, she was welcome in Margaret's home.

The meeting of the farming group which took place on 26 November 1985, was in Rathdrum, roughly twenty-five miles south of her home village of Kilbride. When it was over, Margaret went straight home to the farm, her brown Ford Cortina pulling up outside the two-storey farmhouse sometime after ten o'clock. At that point, Margaret's daughter was already dead within the house, and Margaret's death was minutes away.

The two bodies – strangled and raped – were found the following day by workmen on the farm, and an intensive investigation got under way. Clues were immediately forthcoming. There was no chaos in the house and little evidence of struggle. Extrapolating from this, the gardaí speculated that one intruder, rather than a gang, had been involved, and that Ann had died before her mother returned. Theft did not seem to be the motivation, because although the Cortina had been stolen and was found abandoned outside Wicklow Railway Station, it was likely to have been used for getaway purposes only, and the house still contained items which would have been appealing to a thief. So it seemed that the killer had come on foot and that he might have been on his own.

It was a virtual certainty that he was male and very strong.

Less certain, but very likely, was the probability that Margaret and Ann had known their murderer. This probability, however, did not lessen the fears of local people panicked by the idea of a wandering murderer. The elderly woman who had, with unconscious irony, been offered companionship by Margaret Nolan was one of several who moved into Wicklow town until the murderer was caught.

Reading between the lines of garda comment a couple of days after the murder would have reinforced the idea that the murderer might be a local man. The Cortina had been abandoned at the railway station, but that didn't mean the driver had taken the train out of Wicklow. On the contrary. When found, the car was very much "iced up," an indicator that it had been where it was found for much of the night. Local residents told reporters that the car must have been there before the main group of railway commuters arrived by car the morning after the murder, because if it had not arrived so early, it would have been parked further away from the station itself. So the driver of the Cortina was not likely to have taken the train. What he might have done was walk on the railway line to Rathnew or to Wicklow, knowing that it was a direct route, free from trains in the middle of the night, but also free of observers.

There was no secrecy about the concern of the gardaí and of public figures about this double murder. The Superintendent leading the enquiry asked people to contact the gardaí if anyone in the area had seen anything odd or different. The Minister for Justice, Michael Noonan, TD, echoed this, saying that any scrap of information, no matter how irrelevant it might seem, should be relayed by the public to the gardaí.

"People can be assured that the State will leave no stone unturned to bring these killers to justice, and anyone who may have seen or heard anything at all that might be useful to this major investigation should immediately contact the gardaí," said Minister Noonan.

The Fine Gael man was not the only Minister of the Coalition Government to indicate personal concern. Labour's Liam Kavanagh, a Wicklow man, departed from his script at the opening of a local water scheme to express his shock at the murders and to beg people to give the gardaí any information they had.

Two weeks after the murders, the gardaí, who had by then interviewed almost 2000 people, predicted that they were on the verge of a breakthrough. Not long afterwards, that breakthrough came, and Brian Fortune, a well-built eighteen-year-old with curly dark hair, was charged with the killings.

When Brian Fortune's case came to court in April of the following year, it was distinguished by its brevity, the hearing lasting only four minutes. The teenager stood in self-contained silence as the registrar read out the charge of murder of Margaret Nolan.

"How do you plead, guilty or not guilty?" he was asked.

"Guilty, your honour," was the reply.

Mr Justice Rory O'Hanlon imposed the mandatory sentence: penal servitude for life, recommending psychiatric assessment of Fortune in order to help the Minister for Justice to determine if he, the Minister, should have input into the decision on where the prisoner should be detained. A *nolle prosequi* was entered by the Director of Public Prosecutions to indicate that he had no intention at that time of proceeding against Fortune for the second murder.

The DPP did not make public his reasons, but the likelihood is that the decision was taken to save public money in the light of the fact that Fortune was already due to serve a life sentence for the murder of the mother.

Fortune's counsel said that the young man did not want to cause any further anxiety to his own family or to the family of the murdered women, so there was little point in having his personal background outlined in court. Mr Justice O'Hanlon (who was later to create his own headlines by going public with his personal anti-abortion views in the run-up to a referendum on abortion) agreed that it wasn't necessary to go into further detail. Within minutes, Fortune was on his way back to Mountjoy.

However, if the judge and the counsel for the convicted

man didn't think it necessary to go into background details, the newspapers thought otherwise. The following day, much space was devoted to the fact that Brian Fortune's family and the Nolan family had known each other well, and that he had worked during several summers on the Nolan farm. Fellow workers talked of him as a strong, hard worker. The eldest – and only son – of a family of six, he had left school at fifteen to work on farms, and to win several awards at ploughing championships. His only problem with keeping jobs seemed to be that he had no transport of his own.

When Fortune had worked during the summer months on the Nolan farm, he had stayed in his grandmother's cottage. Mrs Nolan had even bought him a bike so he could move between the cottage and her farm, a distance of about 500 yards, more easily.

It was Brian Fortune's grandmother, in her eighties, who had been told by the dead woman that if she ever felt anxious in her own cottage, she was welcome to come to Margaret Nolan's house and stay with her. So frightened had the grandmother been by the double murder that she had moved into Wicklow town for safety, not knowing that her own beloved grandson was the perpetrator.

For some commentators, while there was no doubt that justice had been done, there was some question that it had been seen to be done, because of the fact that no evidence had been presented in court. The public did not learn how Fortune ended up making his statement to the gardaí, nor was any information about the solving of the crime released after the murderer was convicted. It was believed, but never stated in court, that in the early hours of the morning following the murders, Fortune had been sleepless and distressed, calling to the local garda station just after six, reporting chest pains and asking the gardaí to contact a doctor for him. A doctor reportedly arrived, medicated him and took him back to his grandmother's cottage, but because this was never played out in court, it was impossible to judge how much this incident, if it happened, had later contributed to garda suspicion of Fortune. "It could be argued persuasively that Fortune's guilty plea saved his family and relatives of the Nolans, undue hardship, that nothing would have been gained from lengthy proceedings in which salacious details were relayed for the sole benefit of the newspapers," wrote Sean Flynn, the *Irish Times*'s Security Correspondent at the time. "However, the complete absence of any evidence in the case . . . only served to fuel rumour and innuendo."

Everybody had their own theory as to why Fortune had committed the crimes, but accurate insight from the man himself was not forthcoming. Without information, both on the motivation of the killer and on the methods used to bring him to justice, the public were afforded no opportunity to learn anything from the double tragedy.

His grandmother, devastated, could only talk of him having been "a good, hardworking lad" and of Mrs Nolan as an employer who had been good to him.

"He was a most obliging lad, he'd do anything for me," she said sadly. "It was an awful thing. I don't know in the name of God what happened to him."

FUNERAL AT DAYBREAK

Wife Murder in Dripsey, County Cork

If there is one profession more than any other which is over-represented in the ranks of murderers, that profession is medicine. Any student of murder, asked to spiel off the classic cases, is likely to include Dr Crippen, Dr Buck Ruxton, Dr Neil Cream, whereas it is quite difficult to call to mind three or more architects who are famous for murder. Or physicists, dentists or vets. One crime writer has posited the notion of murder as an affliction of the medical profession in the same way as silicosis is an affliction of miners.

Ireland has produced more than one medical murderer. Northern Ireland produced Dr Adams (see page 53). Cork produced Dr Philip Cross. Romantic notions in his sixties turned the man who looked a little like Abraham Lincoln into a murderer.

Philip Cross, up to then, had been an army physician, spending years in India, and the doctor and his wife had both enjoyed their overseas years. There had been servants and a position, and enough money to keep both. In 1886, the doctor, his wife and their four children were back at Shandy Hall, Dripsey, County Cork, because British Army regulations retired a medical man at sixty. "Philip has the stamina and the physique of a young man," Laura Cross would sadly tell her friends, knowing that the prospect of building up a medical practice in rural Cork was not engaging all of her husband's physical or mental energies. Colds, splinters and chilblains could not compare, as medical challenges, to the serious work required of an army medic. Of course, there was the estate to be attended to, but that bored him, too.

When a distraction came along, it came along in the twenty-year-old shape of a governess for the four children, named Mary Skinner.

Miss Skinner was a daydreamer who had not travelled much. She read as many romances as she could lay her hands on, and was attractive and good-humoured. The children liked her, as did Mrs Cross, who was much nearer the age of the governess than that of her husband. Age-gap notwithstanding, Mary Skinner soon became close to the Doctor. Far too close, in the view of Mrs Cross, who ordered her from the house and in a blind rage told her she wished her joy in finding a new job without a reference. (These days, a reference is a final check on a candidate. At the end of the last century, it was the preliminary qualification. Without an enthusiastic reference from your most recent employer, you had no prayer of another job.)

The dismissal did not put an end to the relationship between the retired army man and the twenty-year-old. Very soon thereafter, Mary was set up in lodgings of her own in Dublin, and was visited by the Doctor whenever he could make it from Cork. Although Mrs Cross was busy with her own social life among the locals and did not tune in to what her husband was up to, Philip did not take long to weary of the travel and of the mendacity. His options were limited. Divorce was not a real possibility; nor was abandonment of wife and offspring to live in sin with his beloved. Anyway, you could not abandon a sick wife and, around this time, Mrs Cross began to feel very iffy. As 1886 moved into 1887, the searing thirst, allied to diarrhoea and vomiting, which afflicted the doctor's wife were turning her into a shadow. A resigned shadow. "He doesn't think I'll last the year," she said of her doctor husband. "He says I have a diseased heart. Phil is troubled . . . "

Not only was Phil troubled, he was garrulous, too, talking to anybody who would hold still about his wife's declining health, except when he had to go to Dublin "on business." Although she seemed to rally a little as the daffodils began to appear that springtime, Mrs Cross's end was near, her physician spouse told friends and neighbours. Those friends and neighbours were bowled over by the gallantry and concern of Dr Cross. His love and kindness to his wife were always in evidence, and his efforts to help her were manifest in the personally prepared doses of medicine he made up for her. He even went to the lengths of calling in a second opinion. The second opinion was a Dr Godfrey, who just happened to be freshly qualified and a cousin impressed to death by the experience and expertise of Dr Cross. Just in case the young medic got ideas about having an independent second opinion, Dr Cross casually dropped his own diagnosis as he led his cousin to examine his wife. "It's typhoid fever, of course," he said.

Dr Godfrey examined the patient and acquiesced with career-building docility. Of course it was typhoid. Absolutely.

Seven days later, screams in the night preceded the death of Mrs Cross early on the morning of 2 June. The screams were heard only by a couple of servants within the house, and so need never have incriminated Philip Cross. But the doctor seemed to have a deathwish directed at himself as well as at his wife, because he now proceeded to take a number of actions which, in their crudity, attracted attention he should have been at pains to avoid.

The timing of the funeral was the first of those actions. Six o'clock in the morning is a weird time for a funeral, and when Dr Cross buried his wife in the pale brightness of a summer dawn, he did it virtually on his own.

Few relatives had been told of her death, and those who knew about it had not expected a funeral at daybreak. He did have a ready answer for critics. Burials in India took place before the sun was up. This might very well be true, some of Mrs Cross's relatives accepted, but it was of minor relevance in Dripsey, where the sun never reached the torrid heat levels associated with India.

If Dr Cross had hoped to conceal from those few mourners who turned up, in the shadowy early morning, the fact that he had buried his wife in a cheaper than cheap coffin and without any costly frills, he had not thought it through. Local gentry quickly heard about the discount obsequies and their early start. Gossip ran throughout the community as people sought to make sense of the caring doctor's strange post-mortem disregard for his younger wife.

Cross had little time to waste on gossip. He had another agenda. The priority was to organise childcare, which he did within ten days, and to depart for London. Less than a fortnight after his wife's death, Dr Philip Cross married Mary Skinner in one of the most lavish weddings possible at St James's Church, Piccadilly. The nuptials made their way into all of the society columns in the newspapers, and some of those newspapers were to be read in Cross's home town. The locals now had more questions than a catechism. Had he married a girl a third of his age? The girl his wife had fired? Why had his wife fired her? Why a cheap funeral for a wife who has given you her life and four children, and a lavish wedding two weeks later? One of the locals who was still impressed by Dr Cross, and who believed that the gossips must be missing some reasonable rationale underpinning the former army man's actions, took pen in hand and wrote to him, filling him in on the bad things being said about him, the questions being asked, and the doubts being expressed.

This missive reached the doctor in mid-honeymoon in London, and he decided to go straight home and face down the begrudgers, arriving roughly three weeks after his wife had died. What he didn't know was that the questions and the doubts had been addressed to more than himself. Inspector Tyacke of the Royal Irish Constabulary had been supplied with a version of the queries forwarded to Cross, and had made a few desultory checks. There had been no post-mortem on the dead woman, he learned. The death certificate or "ticket" had been signed by her husband. Tyacke decided that perhaps there was more than provincial gossip at work here, and asked a local magistrate to order an exhumation of Mrs Cross's body. The order was issued, the shovels went to work, the body was exhumed and the medical men, not including Dr Cross, went to work. The widower bore this invasion of his dead wife's privacy and the slur on his own good name in dignity and silence.

In short order, the pathologist who examined Mrs Cross's remains found proof therein that she had been poisoned, over a period of at least three months, with repeated doses of strychnine and arsenic. The weak heart of which Dr Cross had often spoken as his wife's chief ailment, turned out to have been a fairly sturdy organ. The typhoid fever, which he had persuaded the young doctor to believe must be present, had not been there.

Tyacke, who had taken a considerable personal risk in seeking the exhumation, must have felt at no risk whatever when he ordered the arrest of Cross. The men who detained him heard him ask his sister if she had, as requested, destroyed two bottles "with white powder in them." The sister had apparently done as asked, because no incriminating vessels were ever found to point directly to ownership of the poison which had robbed Mrs Cross of her life. But the prosecution needed no minor props such as bottles filled with white powder. They had more than enough to damn him before a jury at the Munster Assizes.

They were able to prove – and did so at somewhat tedious length – that he and Mary Skinner had lived together in Dublin as Mr and Mrs Osborne, long before Mrs Cross had departed this life. That meant adultery. They were also able to prove that Cross had bought consignments of arsenic in Dublin, telling the dispensing chemist that he planned to use them in sheep-dip.

The verdict of guilty came as no surprise to anybody except perhaps Dr Cross himself. The old army man, who had become shrunken, depressed and silent while awaiting trial, suddenly became contentious, and tried, somewhat late in the day, to prove to Judge Murphy that he could not have put the arsenic into his wife's stomach. Justice Murphy ordered him to silence and sentenced him to death.

Rejected by his new wife, Dr Philip Cross was hanged in January, 1888.

"Incorrigible in Penal Terms, Incurable in Medical Terms"

The First Irish Serial Killer

Ireland has had a number of "multicides": people who killed more than one person at one time. In the eighties, in the west, a young man shot to death his former girlfriend and her mother in a hospital car-park because the girl had decided to end their relationship. In Malahide, earlier in this century, a gardener murdered a complete family because he was about to lose his job with them. (See Prone, *Irish Murders* 1.)

We have yet to join the twin grim trends towards spree-killing and serial-killing which have become a not infrequent crime feature in other countries. Spree-killing is when several victims are killed at one time, having come into contact with the murderer by accident. They are often strangers to him (or her). In Britain, the Hungerford Massacre saw a young gun-freak kill more than a dozen total strangers in the street in less than two hours. In 1966 in Austin, Texas, a man named Charles Whitman murdered his wife and mother, and then, armed with a rifle, climbed to the top of a tower on the campus of the University of Texas, killing sixteen people and wounding almost twice as many before he was picked off by a police marksman.

Serial-killing is quite different, involving repetitious murders spread out over months or years. Ted Bundy, the personable killer eventually executed to much popular celebration in Florida, was one such killer, murdering young women, the total number of whom was never finally calculated, since the authorities in the United States tired of Bundy using, as a ploy to postpone execution, the promise to reveal his involvement in one more unsolved murder in any one of a dozen states of the union.

Serial killers tend to have a number of traits in common. They are young and male for the most part, although a female prostitute in Florida has been convicted of a series of killings involving truck drivers who stopped to pick her up on the highway. They have often sustained severe head injuries as children or young adults, are frequently the unwanted children of drunks or drug-addicts, and frequently suffer from alcohol or drug-addictions themselves. Psychologist Joel Norris, who has published studies of the serial-killer phenomenon, says that the majority of them are physically and psychologically damaged people. (He also notes that many have "obvious physical and congenital defects such as webbed fingers, attached ear lobes, elongated limbs and other abnormalities.")

Serial killers operate best in a society where transient relationships are the norm, where change is constant, and where population is large and diverse. It may be that Ireland is still too small and intimate a community to provide the breeding ground for such killers.

The one Irish serial killer on the record books thus far did his killings, according to himself, in Britain. In August, 1983, Kieran Kelly, an Irish tramp, killed another vagrant in Clapham and was caught and convicted within a year. At the time of his conviction – June, 1984 – Kelly was fifty-four years of age. He was an alcoholic, and had been described by a psychiatrist as "incorrigible in penal terms and incurable in medical terms." When the trial judge vehemently agreed with the psychiatric judgement, he no doubt had in mind the killing that Kelly had done back in 1975, when he had murdered a drinking companion.

If the judge took the psychiatrist seriously, and sentenced Kelly to a life sentence for the killing of the other vagrant, the police took him equally seriously when he told them he was guilty of as many as nine murders in the previous thirty years.

Kelly had left Ireland in 1953, and had been living rough in England ever since, the thirty-something intervening years peppered with one or two convictions every twelve months for drink-related offences. He was tried more than once for murder or attempted murder, because some of his violent outrages were committed in front of witnesses, but convictions were not obtained.

In the mid-1970s, however, Kelly made it rather easier for the police by committing murder while being held in a police cell. At least he made the *detection* easier. It cannot have been easy for the authorities to explain away what one of their charges did to another of their charges while in custody in mid-summer, 1983. That night, Kelly was in a cell with fifty-five-year-old William Boyd and another man. Kelly arrived into the cell carrying a major load of alcohol having been arrested for drunkenness and robbery. Boyd was not a peaceful cellmate. He shouted and swore a lot, until Kelly took his socks and shoelaces and crafted therefrom a ligature, which he then applied around the neck of Boyd, and strangled him to death. One assumes that the third man in the cell had passed out, was too scared of Kelly to intervene, or actively approved of his actions. Whatever the reason, the murder went unimpeded.

This crime was followed by the confession that he had earlier killed up to nine people. Some of them he named. One was Hector Fisher, an elderly printer Kelly had stabbed to death in a churchyard in Clapham almost a decade earlier.

Although police forces, the world over, are glad to have the chance to solve outstanding cases, they are also wary of the vainglorious joy some killers take in claiming every unsolved murder extant as an example of their work. One recent serial killer in the US has claimed to have perpetrated 500 murders, and although the American cops have no doubt that they have a killer on their hands, they have serious reservations about the overwhelming majority of his claimed crimes. So the British police suspected Kelly of exaggerating the number of people his confession had him claiming to have killed. But, having put detectives to work on the confession, they were convinced that he had certainly had a hand in five of the outstanding cases, and that they had enough evidence to charge him with the malicious killing of Hector Fisher. For this he was given the first of two life sentences.

At his trial for the killing of the Irish tramp, the jury heard that he had obsessions about other tramps and had a violent temper. The judge, in passing sentence, expressed the belief that Kelly was too dangerous ever to be released. "This conviction for a second killing confirms that the view of the consultant psychiatrist who says that you are incorrigible in penal terms and incurable in medical terms is plainly right," concluded the judge.

"Goodbye, my Most Adorable, Wonderful, Desirable, Darling Kathleen"

A Death on Howth Head

It's not often that a murder victim is found surrounded by physical clues, but that's what happened on the morning of 28 May 1948, when a woman's body was discovered at Brackenhurst, at the top of Howth Head. A small woman – about 5'2" and perhaps eight stone in weight – she seemed, when first spotted almost hidden in the grass, to be huddled in sleep. In fact, she was dead, with the clues to her death and her killer scattered around her: two newspapers, the *Daily Express* and the *Evening Herald*, carrying the previous day's date, a couple of fountain pens, a ration book with her name on it, a handbag. And a letter, which was more helpful in the investigation of the crime than the writer could ever have imagined.

The missive was addressed to a Mrs Kay Boyne (the dead woman) from a man signing himself "John" with an address in Phibsboro.

As the gardaí read it and returned to it, the letter served as something akin to a checklist, linking the elements of identification, motivation and character together.

The letter started with a civil enquiry as to how "Kay" was feeling after the "ordeal" of an operation on her foot.

(The post-mortem was to find that the nail on a big toe had been removed, and that the dead woman's foot was bandaged.) "I hate to see you ill, you whom I love so dearly, and how it grieves me not to be able to do something for you," the letter went on.

Then came clue number one to the relationship, and ultimately to the murder itself. The writer of the letter was undoubtedly besotted with Kay Boyne, and deeply fearful that his affection was not returned, and that his beloved was likely at any time to finish off the relationship.

"But my darling," he pleaded desperately, "do not give me up but let me prove my love for you and I swear to you that you will never regret the waiting. At the moment I feel crushed and desolate and humbled and have no one to turn to, in a cold and dreary world for comfort but you, my own sweetest little queen. My destiny is in your hands – a live (sic) of love and happiness with you or a live (sic) broken and crushed with anguish without you. I know you are probably fed up with me but please darling give me a chance and I will make up for everything. God knows how I have tried to love and serve you and how I have adored you and will go on loving and adoring and worshipping you – always my own cry is to be near you close to you."

The writer evidently had some capacity to envisage the probable response of his beloved to this abject outpouring. "If you feel sick and feel like scoffing at this letter please don't," he went on pathetically. "Treat me kindly . . . " A couple of sentences later, he had lost confidence even further. "I had better finish," he suggested, "or if this epistle is any longer you will probably get tired reading it."

But before he signed off, "John" inadvertently gave the gardaí who were investigating Kay's murder some more information about their relationship. He was, he wrote, going to leave some sweets with her aunt for her, as she (Kay) had told him (John) never to call to her house, "and you know how afraid I am of you, you who are so tiny and gentle and yet so powerful and so dynamic."

The writer also talked affectionately of "the kids," who turned out to be Kay's two sons, one of them eight years old at the time, the other twelve. Mrs Boyne, it emerged as the day went on, was a widow aged thirty-eight, working as a clerk in Prescott's Dry Cleaners in Grafton Street.

What came through the letter, loud, clear and repetitively, was that "John" was a desperate, clinging and devoted lover of minuscule self-esteem whose moods swung between elation caused by the presence of Kay, and depression in her absence. His letter, filled with references to Kay "soothing his shattered nerves and making his life worth living," ended in a flurry of Christian names and adjectives: "Goodbye my most adorable wonderful, desirable darling Kathleen Patricia Olive, my little 'wee' widow from your own mouldy, loving John."

John turned out to be John Fanning, an unqualified assistant in Hayes Conyngham Robinson's chemists shop in Ballsbridge. The gardaí reached him at Kay's brother's house at half-seven that evening. Kay's brother, with whom she lived since the death of her hairdresser husband, Gerald, had reported her missing at lunchtime that day.

"I'm Inspector Hennon from Howth," one of the investigators told the slim, short, dark-haired Fanning, before asking for information about Kay. Fanning sat down on a sofa and put his head in his hands, remaining silent for about five seconds.

"I met Kay outside the Carlton," he began, going on to

give the gardaí details of how Kay had ended up in what they knew to be a favourite rendezvous for lovers on benign summer nights, Nash Field at Brackenhurst.

First of all, he explained, he had met Kay two years earlier.

"Since then," he told the investigators, "I have met Mrs Boyne at least twice a week. Sometimes three times."

It had been viewing by appointment only; John had telephoned every time, and had tended to meet Kay at the Saxone corner in O'Connell Street, usually on Saturday and Sunday evenings. They had been planning to go to the pictures the night before, specifically to the Carlton. He was there five minutes before Kay arrived, but the movie was a popular one, and they couldn't get into the cinema. Instead, they decided to take a bus-ride out to Howth. The bus was also crowded, Fanning told the gardaí, so crowded that for most of the journey he and Kay had not been able to share a seat, but had been separated. He had slipped her the *Evening Herald* he had bought earlier, and she read it. Although he had both the *Daily Express* and *Time* magazine in his pocket, he didn't read either – one is tempted to guess because they might have distracted him from gazing at the love of his life or thinking about her.

When they arrived in Howth, they set off towards the Royal Hotel. (One of the oddities of this murder is that the victim was required to do a great deal of walking on the night of the crime, which, given the recent surgery on her foot, must have been extremely painful.) During the following hour, each had two small whiskies, topped off in John Fanning's case by a bottle of stout and in Kay Boyne's case by a small port. Thus fortified, the pair set off up the steep road towards Nashville Park, talking about his work and her work, occasionally stopped to rest at a wall which could be leaned against, or a grass bank which could serve as a seat.

While John Fanning was telling the gardaí his story of the two lovers out together in the lovely surroundings of the Howth peninsula, Kay Boyne's body was being examined. She had been found lying on her right side, fully clothed, in a small depression near a fence. The grass beneath the head was bloodstained, as was a portion of a scarf underneath Kay's face, but there was no evidence of a struggle.

What had happened to Kay Boyne had happened too quickly for her to fight for her life. Her hands showed none of the bruising or cuts associated with trying to fight off an assailant. Instead, her face and neck were woefully damaged, with appalling bruising indicative of an attack with a blunt weapon of some kind. On both sides of her face, the bones had been extensively fractured and fragmented. Her real teeth had been broken, as had some false teeth she was wearing.

The signs of manual strangulation were all to be seen on Kay Boyne's body. Her tongue was protruding from her mouth and had been bitten. Blood vessels in the brain were congested, and the lungs were congested, with haemorrhagic spots found especially on the right side. Blood had been inhaled into the windpipe, which suggested that Kay had been battered about the face first, and then strangled. There was no evidence of rape, and Kay had not been pregnant. "From this examination I formed the opinion that the cause of death was shock and asphyxia produced by manual strangulation and blows on the face and head with some blunt or partly blunt instrument," concluded the State Pathologist, who estimated the time of death to have been within an hour or two of midnight on the 27/28 May.

As the State Pathologist was moving on to examine some men's clothing with which he had been supplied, John Fanning was explaining to the guards that when he and Kay had finished their romantic evening on Howth Head, they had fortuitously encountered, around about eleven o'clock, a car full of happily inebriated people who seemed to know Kay and who offered her a lift back to town. For the third time that night, there were too many people around, and they didn't have room in the car for John. No problem, he told them, he'd get the last bus.

It did not seem to bother him that this object of his obsessive passion was departing with a carload of "well-jarred" revellers who were strangers to him. Hmmm, thought the gardaí, impassively noting down the account.

The State Pathologist, moving on from Kay's body to the men's clothing he had been handed, found human bloodstains on them. Quite small human bloodstains on both legs of the trousers. The trousers belonged to John Fanning, who, as time went on, elaborated on his account of what had happened that night. He kept using words like "pleasant," yet some of what he recalled gave indications that Kay Boyne, if she had ever been in love with John Fanning, was now deeply irritated with him. He recounted how, in bending to go under a barbed wire fence on Howth, she had caught her coat, and complained that "my coat is ruined."

"I said, 'I'll buy you another,'" John Fanning told the guards.

"I'll get someone else to buy it, thank you," she had

snapped in response. "I can get plenty to buy for me."

"You are not vexed with me, are you?" asked John, trying to put his arm around her. She pulled away.

Fanning told an improbable story of a pointless quarrel which, according to his version, had sorted itself out for no reason, and then he apparently was overcome with regret at having allowed Kay to go with the carload of semi-strangers. "Oh God," he said, clapping a hand to his head. "Why did I let her go with them?"

He willingly set off with the gardaí for Howth, to show them the place where he had parted company with Kay the previous night. By the time he got there, though, the guards had been informed of the findings of the State Pathologist, and they decided to tell him that the body had been found, that they knew Mrs Boyne had been manually strangled, and to caution him at the same time.

"I want to tell you Mrs Kathleen Boyne is dead," Inspector Hennon told him just before nine o'clock that night.

"Is she? This is terrible," gasped Fanning, bursting into tears.

Holding his face in his hands, he continued to sob for a minute or two, talking to himself in a low voice.

"This is terrible," he kept saying.

"You understand the position?" queried Inspector Hennon. "You appear to have been one of the last people who saw Mrs Kathleen Boyne alive. I therefore caution you."

Another garda asked him how he was feeling.

"I am in a shocking mess," was the reply. "It is strange how the tricks of fate have played on me."

Agitated by the grim news, he still evinced willingness

to take the investigators to the places visited the previous night. The waiter at the Royal Howth Hotel identified him as having been there the night before. Fanning showed the gardaí the field at Brackenhurst, overlooking Howth Harbour, with its fine view, and told them how he had spread out the two newspapers he had brought with him to provide a dry place to sit down. As he talked more, the group of people in the car began to seem more and more like dream figures. Eventually, he was shown the stains on his trousers – trousers he had often packaged up neatly and presented to Kay Boyne, asking her to have them cleaned at her place of work and topping off the package with a love letter. "If I am being detained, I do not wish to say anything until I see my solicitor," he said, adding, in what seems to have been an exculpatory comment on the trouser stains, "in my job I have to deal with a lot of chemicals."

His home was searched, revealing a collection of letters signed "Kay," which established beyond doubt that if John Fanning was infatuated with Kay Boyne, the young widow was trying to break off the relationship, and quite possibly had planned for the night of the twenty-seventh to be the decisive encounter. Kay had probably been glad that the cinema had been crowded, since it would give her a chance to do some straight talking with her soon-to-be-ex-boyfriend. She would not have anticipated that the location suitable for an intimate conversation, because of its quiet isolation, would also be suitable for murder.

The murder happened in springtime. The trial happened in autumn, with John Fanning pleading "not guilty" and giving evidence on his own behalf. He told the court that he and Kay had had a "tiff" in the field at

Brackenhurst and that something had snapped in his brain. Not knowing quite what he was doing, he had grabbed her by the throat. He had also kicked her and kicked her handbag, scattering the contents.

The jury heard him declare that not only was he deeply in love with the dead woman, but he had been very fond of her two children, and had wanted nothing in life more than marriage with her. Although he admitted that she had never been in love with him, she had, nonetheless, promised to marry him when he qualified. He had sat for the assistant's examination in pharmacy the previous October, but hadn't passed, because, he said, his nerves had failed him in the practical test. The month before the murder, he had sat the final pharmacist's exam and failed it. This failure had caused him the worry and depression referred to in the letter he had written to Kay and which had been found near her dead body. "I have been going through hell for the past few weeks," Fanning had written. "Only for your sympathy and kindness I do not know what I would have done. A whole lifetime of service to you would not even repay you."

However, if the failure to pass his exam had depressed John, it may also have put the kibosh on his planned future with Kay Boyne, who seems to have decided that adoration was not enough to build a second marriage on. The trial lasted five days, with the twenty-eight-year-old gazing at the ceiling and displaying no emotion. Dark-suited, bespectacled and swarthy, he listened to his counsel point out that if Fanning had planned this murder with malice aforethought, he had "the whole of Hayes, Conyngham and Robinson's shelves at his disposal." But not only had he not used poison, he had brought no weapon of any kind with him to Howth: "no hammer, no revolver, no bottle or poison," said Sir John Esmonde, SC, who went on to submit that if John Fanning had planned to do away with Kay Boyne, he would scarcely have picked a public place resorted to by as many as six courting couples a night.

Giving evidence on his own behalf, John Fanning became deeply emotional, telling the jury that something had snapped in his head that night, and that he was in "a kind of frenzy or something." Jettisoning the story told to the gardaí of the arrival of a car filled with acquaintances of Kay, he admitted that the tragedy had begun when the couple had a "tiff" in Nash Field.

"I wanted to kiss her goodnight, but she refused," he recounted. "I put my arms around her and tried to kiss her and both of us fell to the ground on the slope . . . the next thing I had my hands around her throat. I kept on squeezing and I could not take my hands away. I had to kind of drag them away and then she fell limp."

There had been no intention of doing her harm, he claimed. He had not known what he was doing. Even after she was lifeless, and he had felt for her heartbeat to confirm this, he had kicked her body a number of times. He had only a faint, hazy recollection of how he had got down the road from the field.

Under cross-examination, Fanning admitted that Kay had taken a dim view of his not passing his exams. Their quarrel had started in a small way. She was going on holiday, she told him, and she planned to have a good time. In retaliation, he told her that he would "get someone else" while she was away, and have a good time himself. If that was his plan, she said, they might as well call the whole thing off right then. But, Fanning was eager to point out, this kind of minor battle was a constant factor in their relationship. It had happened umpteen times before and had always been patched up after a few days.

It took an hour and forty minutes for the jury to return a verdict of guilty. Probably because there was no evidence of premeditation, the jury added a recommendation to mercy. They did not find Fanning insane, although medical evidence had been given at the trial that Fanning had one rare condition called "dextro cardia," in which the main organs of the body are transposed. John Fanning was the living contradiction to the metaphorical observation that "his heart is in the right place." His heart was in the wrong place, occupying the right side of his chest. The medical officer at Mountjoy stated bluntly that "this condition is not admitted to have any deleterious effect on the general or mental health," and this was generally accepted as outweighing the evidence of a doctor brought in by the defence to state that this situation, where the liver sat where the heart should sit, "was liable to react mentally on the affected person."

Having heard verdict and recommendation, the judge then asked John Fanning if he had anything to say before sentence was passed on him. Trembling as he grasped the dock rail, the young man spoke in a low but clear voice.

"I have nothing to say."

Mr Justice Davitt said that he was in complete agreement with the verdict, which was, he said, the only one possible in the circumstances. Donning the black cap, he delivered sentence.

"The Sentence and Judgement of the Court are and it is ordered and adjudged that you John Fanning be taken from the bar of the court where you now stand to the prison whence you last came and that on Wednesday the tenth day of November in the year of our Lord one thousand nine hundred and forty eight you be taken to the common place of execution in the Prison in which you shall be then confined and that you be then and there hanged by the neck until you be dead and that your body be buried within the walls of the Prison in which the aforesaid Judgement of Death shall be executed upon you. May the Lord have Mercy on your soul."

In prison, Fanning didn't talk about the murder, and was a docile prisoner who seemed mildly depressed. In November came a letter in classic civil service language, issued from the private secretary to the Minister for Justice to the County Registrar at the Four Courts.

I am desired by the Minister for Justice to refer to the case of John Fanning, who, at the Central Criminal Court on the 22nd ultimo, was found guilty of murder, and to inform you that the President, on the advice of the Government, has commuted to penal servitude for life the death sentence passed by the court in this case.

THE JUDGE'S DAUGHTER AND
THE RAF MAN

Death in the Grounds of Her Own Home

It was in the small hours of the morning that the police constable arrived at the home of the Ulster High Court judge at Whiteabbey, a village near Belfast.

The date was the thirteenth of November 1952. It was very dark, and, in the words of the constable, there was a "mizzle" (soft rain) falling. The house dogs responded to the constable's arrival.

"Is that the police?" came the voice of Mr Justice Curran, over their barking.

As Constable Rutherford opened his mouth to identify himself, there were shouts from another part of the grounds. The house-owner and the policeman took off at a run in the direction of the shouts, helped by the light from a torch being shone on an object at the foot of a tree.

The "object" was the body of Patricia Curran, the judge's daughter. She was lying on her back, in the grounds of her own home, dead. Her college books were stacked neatly nearby. Her shoes were missing. Her body showed almost forty wounds – so many that at first it was assumed that a blast from a shotgun had killed her. Later, it was to emerge that the wounds had been frenziedly delivered with a knife, and that eight of them would have killed her. She had been found by her brother, who went out to search when she hadn't returned home the previous evening according to her normal routine.

Patricia Curran's life had been a respectable and orderly one. She was nineteen, and had entered Queen's University a few months before her death, travelling to and from Belfast by bus.

If she knew she would be returning home after dark, she would always telephone home in advance so that a member of the family could come down to the road to meet her, since her home was at the end of a six-hundred-yard driveway which led through trees and shrubbery. It was a journey later described in court as one that "no young girl would relish. One that a girl would not go on alone unless it was absolutely necessary."

On the finding of Patricia's body, two sets of activities ensued. One was the examination of the body itself, with its horrific injuries, twenty-one of them to the chest of the teenager. Both of Patricia's lungs had been partially collapsed by stabs to the chest, and her heart had been reached twice by the weapon. The doctors examining the body concluded that death was due to shock caused by haemorrhage from multiple stab wounds inflicted on the chest, scalp, abdomen and right thigh.

At the same time, the police were already developing a picture of Patricia's movements on the day of her death. On the morning of the twelfth, she had left home as usual and attended lectures at the university. Because she had a free afternoon, she had met another first-year student for tea. This student – a young man – had left her to the bus station and seen her board the five o'clock bus for

Whiteabbey, her home village.

Two passengers on the bus later remembered that she had been on her own, and had seen her disembark and head towards the gates of her home. They were the last people the police were able to find who had seen Patricia alive on that November evening.

As darkness fell and no word came from Patricia, her family were at first puzzled, then uneasy and then frankly anxious. Shortly before two o'clock in the morning, the Whiteabbey police were telephoned from the house, and Patricia's father and brother started to scour the grounds of the house in the hope of locating her. Just as the policeman arrived in response to the phone call, Patricia's brother Desmond located the body.

It was a clueless murder. Patricia had not been raped, although the fact that her clothes were torn suggested that her attacker had planned a sexual assault. On the other hand, the neatly stacked college books suggested that she had put them down herself and perhaps stopped to talk to someone she knew. When that person, whether they were friend or stranger, had turned violent, Patricia had put up what was described as "a stern resistance." The evidence for this was simple and vivid: among other pointers, the hands and glass had been torn completely off her wristwatch and it had ended with its face turned to the inside of her arm.

The body had been dragged some forty feet away from the main avenue into the shrubbery, presumably to hide it temporarily. There was a blood-strained track, showing how Patricia had been pulled from the spot where she had been stabbed. Nobody had seen Patricia after she entered the grounds of the family home. So the police started on what turned out to be 40,000 interviews in order to find the person – it was assumed to be male – who had stabbed her to death. Friends were questioned. People from Whiteabbey village were questioned.

Judge Curran, the dead girl's father, made an appeal to the public on behalf of his family: "We plead with everyone who has the slightest piece of information that might help to give such information to the police . . . we are concerned to see that this foul murderer is brought to justice, not through any spirit of vengeance, but to ensure that other people's daughters may be safe. We keep asking ourselves who will be the next victim . . . "

One piece of evidence which proved to be significant in establishing the timing of the murder was provided by a twelve-year-old newsboy. This boy normally delivered papers to various people in the Whiteabbey district after he finished school, his customers including Justice Curran, the dead girl's father.

On the evening of the crime, the boy headed off at about half-past five, clutching his bundles of papers and heading for Glen House, the Curran home. Because the Glen House avenue was so long, the Currans had put a mailbox about halfway down, to save postmen and newspaper boys having to travel the full journey to the front door. As the newspaper boy marched up the avenue towards this halfway point, he heard the nearby factory horn indicating that it was now a quarter to six. He delivered the paper and had turned to come down the avenue again when he heard a noise in the bushes about sixty yards from where Patricia Curran's body was later found. Something about the noise terrified the twelve-year-old, who took to his heels and ran. The sound, he said, was totally unlike the noises of birds he had been hearing up to that point. It was a noise like that of somebody's foot moving in the leaves.

The RUC, knowing, as they now did, that Patricia's body was already stiff by the time it was found in the small hours of the following morning, had to examine the possibility that what the newspaper boy had heard was some part of the murderous assault or of the concealing of the body. They factored it into their thinking as they went about their investigations.

By Monday the seventeenth, a week after the murder, the RUC stood back from the energetic enquiries they had been pursuing and bluntly admitted to themselves and to others that they were without motive and without weapon. The Inspector General of the RUC then announced that Scotland Yard had been called in, not to take charge of the case, but to co-operate with the Ulster police. It was the first time Scotland Yard officers had been called into Northern Ireland on a murder case. One of the "Yard" men who arrived was Superintendent John Capstick, who had specialised in inquiries into murders, jewel robberies and horse-doping. Much quoted in optimistic publicity in advance of his arrival was the fact that he had, the previous year, caught the killer of a seventy-two-year-old man just seven days after opening the investigation.

During the week after the arrival of the two Scotland Yard advisers, what was described as "an inch by inch" search was made of the area where the murder had happened, and the questioning extended in wider and wider circles. One of the locations where questions were asked was in the nearby Edenmore RAF station. First time around, the detectives asked the airmen in the station to

account for their movements between eleven and midnight
on the night of the murder.

After the newsboy's revelations, they were enquiring
about a quite different time. On the second visit, detectives
were asking the men to account for their movements
between five and six p.m. on the same evening.

It was at this point that suspicion began to fall on one
Iain Hay Gordon. Gordon was a twenty-year-old Scot, and
if his own account of his movements was to be believed,
he had no problems at all, and no association with the
murder. Gordon could account for every minute of his time
between five and six on the day of the murder. The
problem was that, even though he was able to point out
particular locations where he had been during the vital
hour, Gordon obviously felt his position would be
strengthened if he had someone else to support his claims,
and he therefore managed to stimulate the initial suspicion
of himself by trying to produce a witness to testify to his
location during that hour.

As a potential provider of the desired alibi, Gordon had
picked (among others) a teleprinter operator at the RAF
station named Aircraftman Douglas P Walsh. Aircraftman
Walsh knew Gordon and about a fortnight after the murder
had been drinking in a nearby hostelry when Gordon
arrived and planted himself at Walsh's table, asking the
proprietor of the pub for an evening paper. Inevitably,
there was coverage in that paper of the recent murder and
of the vast span of investigation being undertaken by the
police, aided by Scotland Yard. (The murder also attracted
much coverage in the British newspapers, which caused
considerable irritation in the area, as local people did not
like to see this exceptional murder plastered all over the

more sensational daily and Sunday pre-tabloids.)

The two men idly discussed the murder, and the pub owner and her husband joined in. Later, the two RAF men set off for their base together, continuing the chat. As they passed a radar workshop, Gordon opined that if he had a friend – a very good friend – and that friend was in trouble, than he, Gordon, would be prepared to lie for him. Walsh's response was not, evidently, what Gordon had hoped for: "I told him that was all wrong and that such a thing could not be done."

What was significant about Gordon's attempted fabrication of an alibi was that he was preparing it before he was questioned about the actual time of the murder. In other words, before the police questions established that they now presumed Patricia to have been killed much earlier than they had initially supposed, Iain Hay Gordon was already beavering away to cover his tracks for the period during which the murder took place.

Not only was he beavering away, he could not keep his mouth shut about what he was trying to achieve. When another acquaintance of his told him that he could testify only to having seen Gordon around four-thirty on the evening of the crime, Gordon muttered desperately that he couldn't get anyone to give the evidence he needed. The acquaintance shrugged. "If you are down at the police, don't say I was asking you anything," Gordon then requested.

Gordon had been a friend of Patricia's brother, Desmond, the young man who had found the body, and had been to the family's home a number of times. Gordon confirmed to the police that he had been to Curran's for dinner at least three times. "I know very little about Patricia

Patricia O'Toole, murdered in the Dublin
mountains in 1991 (pp 1–14)

26-year-old Private Sean Courtney,
found guilty in 1992 of murdering
Patricia O'Toole

An artist's impression of John Fleming, the "Northside Playboy" of 1930s Dublin, who brutally murdered his wife, having promised marriage to his pregnant girlfriend (pp 29-52)

Main door of Mountjoy Prison, Dublin

Dr Bodkin Adams, the Northern doctor who operated a lethal scam between 1936 and the mid-1950s, encouraging wealthy patients to be more than generous to him in their wills. Once the wills were signed, the patients tended to die suddenly. (pp 53-63)

Mrs Ball's Austin car found dumped at Corbawn Lane, Shankill. Her son Edward had spent much of that night in the car with his murdered mother's body before disposing of it in the sea. (pp 64-78)

The staircase of Mrs Ball's home. Her body was dragged downstairs by her son. Pieces of paper indicate bloodstains left.

The Central Mental Hospital, Dundrum, Dublin

Pierrepoint, the British executioner who often came to Ireland to carry out hangings

Gardaí at the scene of Kay Boyne's murder, pointing to the dead body, the previous day's newspaper belonging to the victim and Kay's handbag (pp 96-107)

43 Slandan Aala
8. AM May 25th

My dearest darling Kay,

My father and I enjoyed the play last night very well. My father said to thank you for her ~~ticket the play room.~~ As for my part, well I liked it but if you had been near me I would have enjoyed it very much more. I had to keep very quiet and missed that something which I usually feel with you. We got a very nice seat in the centre and ~~had~~ we had a bottle each after as one in my condition needs some stimulent to me going when I am without the best stimulent of all my little wee widow.

I am enclosing pants to get cleaned as arranged.

I will have to finish now as I am writing this in a hurry. So excuse short scribble.

I will keep all till I see you to-morrow night. Oh darling how I am yearning for that stick of dynamite.

Very best love.
my darling.
John.

The last letter the besotted John Fanning wrote to Kay Boyne a few days before he murdered her

Judge Curran's daughter, Patricia, who was stabbed in the grounds of her home near Belfast on 12 November 1952 (pp 108-126).

RAF man, Iain Hay Gordon, convicted of murdering Patricia Curran, continued to protest his innocence long after being released

and absolutely nothing about her private life," he told the investigators. "She struck me as being very intelligent, full of life, and the last person anyone would wish to harm. They seemed a very happy family and on the best of terms."

A black eye complicated Gordon's determination to prove himself uninvolved with the murder. The aircraftman told the police that the shiner "was more of an accident than anything else," and had happened when he was messing around the billet with another airman.

But the black eye was just one element in a steadily tightening network of clues pointing to Gordon as Patricia's killer. Another clue was provided by "the woman in black," Mrs Hettie Lyttle, who worked at a nearby weaving factory. Having left the factory at around six on the evening of the murder, she had been about to cross the road close to the gateway into the Currans' lands when a boy came down the avenue from Glen House. He was very pale. She described him to the police, who then pulled Gordon into an identity parade, making sure that the young man was happy both with his position in the parade and the way all the other men in the parade were dressed; there were no give-away clues. Mrs Lyttle took a couple of moments to make up her mind, then moved forward and put her hand on Gordon's shoulder.

As November edged into December, however, a dramatic development happened which took much of the heat off Iain Hay Gordon. That development was the flight to Manchester of one of the Scotland Yard men, together with an RUC inspector, to interview a man in custody there who had made a confession in regard to the Curran murder.

It was a distraction of short duration. The two detectives questioned the Manchester suspect over three hours, during which time he inadvertently proved his own innocence by his self-evident lack of understanding of the terrain in which the murder had taken place. The detectives pointed this out to him; he apologised for wasting their time and was hauled off to be charged with theft. They headed back to Northern Ireland, where a £1,000 reward had been posted.

While they were in Manchester, the investigations around Whiteabbey had continued, unabated. Unabated, too, was Iain Hay Gordon's unintentional pointing of the finger at himself. He asked several colleagues to tell the police that he had been seen by them on the night of the twelfth. To a man, they refused, pointing out that they hadn't seen him on that evening.

"You're a nice lot of friends," he complained. "None of you will say that you saw me on the night of the twelfth."

His friends pointed out to him that it was rather too serious an issue to lie about.

He couldn't seem to stop talking about the murder. Patricia's brother, Desmond, was just one of the people to whom he talked. Desmond believed him "obsessed" by the killing. If he was, that obsession robbed him of any sensitivity: he talked to Desmond with wonderment about why the killer would have stabbed Patricia so many times when "the fourth blow killed her." Having delivered himself of this strange observation, he then wanted to know if Patricia's diaries had carried any reference to him. Patricia had kept a diary up to two days before the murder.

Almost a month after the murder, Gordon confessed. It

was a confession which started with a series of apologies:

"I am very sorry for having killed Patricia Curran. I had no intention whatever of killing the girl. It was due solely to a black-out. God knows as well as anybody that the furthest thing from my mind was to kill this girl. I throw myself on the mercy of the law and ask you to do the best you can for me, so that I can make a new start in life. I am very sorry to have caused distress to the Curran family. I am sorry for the worry and distress I have caused my dear father and mother and I ask my parents' forgiveness. If I am spared I shall redeem my past life."

Then, in a note of bathos, he added: "I have felt run-down for some time."

Gordon told the police that he had left Edenmore Camp in civilian clothes just after five, and had encountered Patricia on the road between the post office and her house. They had greeted each other and she had then asked him to escort her up the avenue because it was getting dark. Gordon said he could quite understand her fear, because the tall trees at the side of the avenue met at the top, shutting out the dwindling evening light. "After we had walked a few yards, I either held her left hand or arm as we walked along," his account continued. "She did not object and was quite cheerful. We carried on walking . . . until we came to the spot where the street lamps' light does not reach. It was quite dark there and I said to Patricia, 'Do you mind if I kiss you?' or words to that effect."

According to Gordon's own account, Patricia was less than enthusiastic about this suggestion, but "consented in the end," possibly because she realised that she was almost equidistant from the road and from her home, and very vulnerable to this young soldier. "I kissed her once or twice to begin with and she did not object," Gordon went on. "She then asked me to continue escorting her up the drive. I did not do so, as I found I could not stop kissing her."

When Gordon began to maul the girl, she struggled and protested, indicating that if he did not let her go, she would tell her father.

From this point, Iain Hay Gordon's confession (not unlike those of serial killer Ted Bundy) moved into the hypothetical mode. "I believe I stabbed her once or twice," he said vaguely, saying he couldn't be sure what kind of knife he had used. "I may have caught her by the throat to stop her from shouting," he added. "I may have pushed her scarves against her mouth to stop her shouting."

It was all very hazy to him, he said. He must have remained hidden when he heard footsteps (probably the newspaper boy) on the driveway. "As far as he knew," he then crossed the road and tossed the knife into the sea. Back at the barracks, he cleaned Patricia's blood from his trousers. "I must have done this, but I do not quite remember," he said.

When charged with the murder, Iain Hay Gordon said, "It was not a wilful murder."

Wilful or not, it was a horrific crime, and one which caused a huge stir, north and south of the border and in Britain, when Gordon came to trial early in the following year. Every seat in the Crown Court at Crumlin Road, Belfast, was filled when the young Scot, who had turned twenty-one in police custody, was tried. Special press seats had to be provided in the jury-in-waiting box for a corps of more than thirty reporters from all over Britain and Ireland. There was even a reporter present from a New York detective magazine. Special telephones had to be installed for the duration.

When arraigned, Gordon, watched by his mother and father, pleaded not guilty. Legal battles took place about the admissibility of his detailed confession (and further battles were to take place long after the court case had concluded) but at the time, the Lord Chief Justice held that the statement was admissible. "I can," he said, "find nothing in the evidence to show that it was procured by promises or threats or any form of coercion, direct or indirect."

The confession was a key part of the prosecution case against the accused. The Attorney General went to some pains to ram home to the jury that Gordon had never been more than six or seven hundred yards from the scene of the crime around the time it was known to have been committed. Gordon's repeated attempts to get other servicemen to lie for him were recounted in the courtroom, as was the story of his initial meeting with Patricia's brother, which had taken place in a church attended by the two men. That meeting had led to a series of civil invitations to lunch and to discussions between the two on moral rearmament.

Desmond Curran told of how, after the murder, Gordon had sought him out to discuss various aspects of the killing with him. Patricia's brother had speculated aloud about how the murderer's conscience must be affecting him. Gordon, in response, had spoken of the multiple murderer Charles Peace, who had confessed to his killings only when he was dying. He also shared with the dead girl's brother his theories about the murder, and wondered why the murderer had gone on to stab her so many times when she had died at the fourth blow.

How, asked Desmond, did Gordon know she had died then?

"Wasn't it in the paper?" asked Gordon.

To which, of course, the answer was: no, it was not in the paper.

When HA M'Veigh, QC, rose to start his ninety-minute outline of the case for the defence, he stated that Gordon was insane in the legal sense. He was suffering from hypoglycaemia – a condition in which there is a dearth of blood sugar in a person's system – and from schizophrenia. The hypoglycaemia claim was an early example of a "dietary" defence which has most frequently been used, in the last twenty years, in the United States.

The QC also spoke of a severe head injury experienced by Gordon only a couple of years beforehand, when he had fallen and cracked his head on some steps. As a result of that accident, he had been taken to the Royal Victoria Hospital, where a fracture of the skull was diagnosed, along with some brain damage.

As his counsel spoke, Gordon wept in the dock. The lawyer promised a "saga of misery" about the accused man and various witnesses, then delivered that saga, starting by putting Brenda Gordon, his mother, in the witness-stand.

His mother explained to the court that Iain Hay Gordon had been born in Burma. His father was an engineer employed by the Burmah Oil Company. The child was the only European youngster in the area and had been a lonely child, nervous and highly strung. Because there was no suitable school, the family had sent him, at six, to a Scottish boarding school and returned to Burma without him.

The trauma this apparent abandonment must have caused to an already sensitive and troubled child may have explained why, in school, Iain was odd and apparently friendless.

His youth was to be subject to even more disruption. At the outbreak of war, about the time of Dunkirk, Mrs Gordon flew home from Burma and brought Iain back out there, in spite of the fact that there was no European school available for the child's education. In 1943 the Japanese invaded Burma, and mother and child spent three days in an airfield waiting to be evacuated to India. The father had to stay behind and for some time, neither Mrs Gordon nor her son knew whether Gordon senior had perished or was still alive.

In India, Mrs Gordon contracted malaria and was taken to hospital. Another apparent abandonment ensued for the Gordon child, who was left in the care of children, and who promptly lost all of his hair – whether through tension or through some disease was never finally established. "Living among refugees without a parent near him," his QC suggested, "surely . . . was enough to upset anybody's mind."

The next step in this "saga of misery" was when Iain Hay Gordon, like his mother, contracted malaria, after which they both embarked on a voyage to Britain which lasted three months and which was fraught with hardship, due to food shortages, and terror, due to U-boat alarms. Adults on the ship stayed drunk as continuously as supplies permitted.

Intoxication distanced the horrors of the voyage, not least of which was the fact that, as the ship was one of a convoy, it was possible to see, each morning, that one or more ships from the convoy had disappeared during the night.

If Iain had been regarded as "funny" when he was a small child in a boarding school, he was regarded as frankly peculiar at a later school, and given the nickname "Crackers". He had a talent for running, but what was most remembered about his athletic outings was one mile-long race, when he was only eighty yards from home and about forty yards in the lead. He looked behind him, stopped, waited until the others came up to him and then ran on again, stopping once again at a later stage to let the boy immediately behind him pass him out.

Despite his peculiarities, Gordon had joined the RAF in 1951. There, he was seen to be easily embarrassed and was quickly flustered into blushing or tears. His over-reaction to any kind of reprimand or discipline was noted by his superiors, who consoled themselves with the fact that he was a willing boy who was due to be with them for a fairly limited time. (Mrs Gordon had earlier seen this extreme reaction to criticism, when Iain had flown into a wild temper and pushed his fist through a window, smashing the glass and yelling "I can't stand it," before becoming enveloped in a white-faced silence.)

The RAF could not figure out his lack of concentration, which would see him listening to simple instructions, racing away to fulfil them, only to have to "telephone home" to base to have them repeated, because the second step in a pattern of instructions always escaped him.

Even though the defence portrayed Gordon's confession as having been induced as a result of high-pressure questioning on irrelevant but upsetting subjects (like his sexual preferences), the major effort went into proving that if the young Scot *had* committed the crime, then he had done it when not responsible, due to insanity. The jury were provided with a considerable amount of medical evidence about the state of Gordon's mind.

In closing, Mr M'Veigh asked the jury to bear in mind the number and indiscriminate nature of the injuries dealt Patricia Curran by Iain Hay Gordon. "What sort of mind do you think the person had who did that?" he asked. "Was it a mind from which direction and control and will had been removed?"

It took just under two hours for the jury to decide that Gordon was guilty but insane. The Lord Chief Justice promptly addressed Gordon, telling him that the sentence of the court was "that you be kept in strict custody until Her Majesty's pleasure is known." He then discharged the jury, exempting them from further service for fifteen years.

When reporters raced from the courthouse with the news, a crowd outside, swelled to more than a thousand by the expectation of the verdict on this exceptional case, gave the result a huge cheer. The cheer continued in waves throughout the bystanders as each group heard what the jury had decided.

The Scotland Yard men packed up and went home, leaving the air thick with compliments about the high standards of the RUC. But that was by no means the end of the Patricia Curran murder case.

The first problem posed by Gordon's conviction was the location of his place of custody. Gordon's parents were anxious to have him committed to some institution near to their home in Scotland, so that they could visit him frequently. However, there was at the time no statutory authority under which Gordon could be removed out of the jurisdiction in which his trial had taken place. Special legislation would have had to be introduced to deal with this unprecedented situation.

When it was made known that he would be serving his time and undergoing treatment at the Holywell Hospital in Antrim, there was local protest. People who lived near the mental hospital disapproved of the incarceration of the murderer there, and believed that non-violent patients would be reluctant to go to an institution housing such a violent man. Resolutions were passed by both Antrim Rural District Council and the Town Commissioners protesting strongly about the issue.

However, there he went and there he stayed, in spite of public predictions that people in and around Holywell would have to keep the doors of their houses "barred from morning till night" as a result.

Gordon's mother, however, never believed her son to be guilty, and for more than four years paid a private detective to amass information on which she based a petition for her son's release, directed at Britain's Home Secretary, WWB Topping.

That petition landed on Topping's desk in 1958, six years after Patricia Curran's death. It was rejected. "I need not say that I am dismayed," said Mrs Gordon, who had sold her house to pay for the investigations. "Iain is not a murderer and I object to anyone calling him so."

Mrs Gordon had nothing but praise for the doctors and staff in Holywell.

A report in 1958 said that Gordon was no longer insane, but he was not then released, because, as the authorities pointed out, other factors, including the gravity of the original crime, had to be taken into account. It was not until late in 1960 that Iain Hay Gordon was released from that hospital into the custody of his parents.

Three years later, Iain, now in his mid-thirties, who was working in a manual job in Glasgow, said that although he didn't want to cause any more pain to the Curran family, he was still seeking to clear his name. "My life since the case has been no life at all," he said. "I don't think I can begin to live normally until the whole thing is cleared up."

The Gordons had kept in touch with "a small group of people in Belfast," who were said to be concerned about some of the methods used to convict him.

When Ludovic Kennedy's book about the 10 Rillington Place murders created an enormous stir, eventually leading to the clearing of Timothy Evans, who had been hanged for the murder of his wife and daughter, those who believed Gordon had been wrongly convicted ensured that Kennedy received all the papers on the case. He wrote to the *Sunday Times* about it in 1968. "It is now, I think, obvious to all that Gordon was neither guilty nor insane in relation to the crime of which he was convicted," said Kennedy's letter, "and it is an appalling thing he should have been harried by the Glasgow police in relation to two murders that have recently taken place there."

Likening the Gordon case to that of Timothy Evans, Ludovic Kennedy claimed that in both cases, conviction rested solely on confessions "obtained by the police in the most dubious circumstances."

"My own view was that Gordon's 'confession' was quite unreliable and in this I was supported by the late Lord Burkitt, to whom I showed the papers at the time."

The Home Office tetchily responded to this by

indicating that inquiries into verdicts of many years previously were not normally instituted on foot of a letter to the papers.

Gordon now maintained that he had been brainwashed by the police into signing a confession. Two years later, seventeen years after his conviction, it was announced that Gordon, by then a warehouseman in Glasgow, would be appearing on BBC 1's *Personal Choice* programme in an interview with Ludovic Kennedy which was to cover the police handling of the young soldier's interrogation.

A week later, it was announced that the BBC had taken the programme off schedules and "looked at it again because of various problems involved."

The BBC action was believed to have followed a letter from the then Ulster Prime Minister, Major Chichester-Clarke, protesting about the resurrection of the tragic event.

Any hopes that Iain Hay Gordon's case might become a *cause célèbre* to match that of Evans or Hanratty died away, and the verdict against him for the murder of the judge's daughter stands to this day.

"NEXT TIME IT WILL BE A CLEAN CUT"

The Torso in the Bog

Every year, more than a thousand people go missing in Ireland. Some are lost at sea. Some are people running away from a home life they no longer want. The majority of missing persons are located as a result of routine enquiries by the gardaí. They're found, alive or dead, in the area or further away.

But when, coming up to Christmas 1941, the gardaí in the Tullamore Depot received a missing person report on Laurence Kirwan, it was a problem that did not lend itself to a fast or easy solution. Laurence was missing about a week before the gardaí were told about it. He had left home and had not returned.

The gardaí visited the farmhouse Laurence was sharing with Bernard, his thirty-three-year-old elder brother, to ask if Bernard had any notion of Laurence's present whereabouts. "He's inside," said Bernard.

Surprise from the gardaí. A double-take and quick correction of the slip of the tongue from Bernard. "Well, no," he amended. "Someone from Ballinamore said he's gone to Kildare to my aunt's."

The gardaí, accepting this for the nonce, told Bernard to get his brother to give them a call when he arrived home.

That Bernard seemed to be getting his information about the man with whom he shared a house, from "someone in Ballinamore" was not considered a great surprise. Bernard and Laurence were not speaking and had made no secret of it.

Bernard's life-story was a somewhat slanted version of Robert Graves's adage that "Home is where, when you have to go there, they have to let you in."

Laurence, his brother, had felt forced to let Bernard in when the elder brother arrived on his doorstep after a spell in prison, but he didn't like having to accommodate him for a number of reasons, including the fact that he had taken over control of the family farm and had no need of an extra hand, since he already had a workman named Foran working for him. The welcome extended to Bernard was, accordingly, something less than warm. For a while, Laurence wouldn't even let him sleep in the place, but eventually caved in on that one, contenting himself with giving Bernard as little food as possible – more on this later – and even less money for work done on the farm.

The elder brother did not take any of this lying down. About a month after his arrival, he took himself off to Dublin for a holiday, financing the trip by means of fifteen pounds nicked from Laurence. Understandably, when he came back, relations between the two were more, rather than less, strained.

Bernard, the elder brother, had returned home in June, 1941 after a chequered career. Often described as "too clever by half," he had, in his twenties, decided to go in for mail robbery. If this crime category evokes mental images of Stetson-hatted riders forcing trains to stop and making off with canvas bags, the pictures do not quite match

Bernard's approach. He did it by blasting the tyres off the bicycle of a postman on his round and making off with the mailbag. He had then secreted the worthwhile contents of the bag in the hollow steel tubes of his own bicycle frame. All of this ingenuity notwithstanding, he was caught for the crime, convicted, and sentenced to seven years penal servitude. At the time of his return to his brother's house, he was a convict on licence, which was the contemporary equivalent of parole. He was also regarded by the gardaí as an unsuccessful, but nonetheless shrewd, calculating and cool crook.

The local gardaí knew him well. They were almost friendly with him. So when Laurence disappeared, they were not surprised when Bernard gave them every assistance short of actual help.

They learned the miserable details of the brothers' life together. How, within three months of Bernard's arrival, Laurence had taken to locking up all food after every meal, so that if he was hungry, Bernard was forced to seek extra sustenance from his sister, who lived not far away. This, understandably, led to friction, which in turn led to violence. "Jack, get up, he's after stabbing me with a knife," was the cry that roused Foran, the workman, from sleep one morning. As Foran stumbled from his bed, Laurence tottered into the employee's room, blood pouring from a deep wound in his right hand. The wound, he told Foran, had been made by Bernard, who had tried to murder him by stabbing him in the throat.

Laurence's life was not endangered by the hand-wound, but Bernard, who claimed the attack had been made by Laurence and the wound delivered when he, Bernard, had defended himself, indicated that next time around, the younger brother might not get off so lightly. "If he ever attacks me again, it will be his last time," he announced. "Next time, it will be a clean cut."

What passed, with the Kirwans, for normal domestic life, then resumed. But Laurence's habit of locking away the food began to be less effective, and he suspected that Bernard had acquired a key in some way. More radical action was required, so he shifted the food supplies from the kitchen cupboard with its now useless lock, storing them instead in the boot of his car.

A man of Bernard's convoluted and criminal intelligence was not to be bested by this kind of measure, and in no time at all, the boot of the ten-horsepower Ford, bought second-hand during the summer, was no longer impregnable.

How had Bernard done it? The soap told the story. A neighbour called to Laurence to ask for the loan of a bar of soap, the request suggesting that although Laurence would go to the most mean-minded lengths to prevent his brother getting more than what Laurence regarded as his bare entitlement of food, he was relatively open-handed with neighbours. The soap was presented to the neighbour, who, turning it over, was intrigued to find the perfect impression of a key. The neighbour showed the neat depression to Laurence. Laurence went for his key-ring. Off came the key to the luggage compartment of the Ford. Into the impression it went – and fitted perfectly. Now Bernard's method of getting extra food was transparently obvious. The incident revealed another aspect of the multi-faceted mind of Bernard. He could devote time, thought and creativity to the development of a solution, yet leave the clues to that solution sitting where his brother and a neighbour could find them without effort.

The duplication of the key further exacerbated the sickness of the relationship between the two brothers. As the winter drew in, normal farm work continued in frozen silence. In November, Laurence could tot up £50 earned from the sale of four cattle, funds earned by reaping corn, spraying potatoes and selling turf. He was a good earner, and careful with money; the sort of man who would go to the bother of cycling rather than driving to the nearest town to return flour sacks purchased for the transport of goods in order to get a refund of a few shillings.

On the day after Laurence had made the trip to get the money back on the sacks, Foran, the workman, arrived into the brothers' home in the small hours of the morning, fresh from a dance, to see food on the table. Knowing Laurence's food fetish, he expressed surprise. "Lar is gone on holiday," Bernard proffered non-committally, making Foran a cup of cocoa. Foran drank the cocoa contentedly, undisturbed by Laurence's absence, since the man was, like himself, often out late on a Saturday night. True, Bernard was wearing an overall and rubber boots belonging to Laurence, but that was Bernard's business. True, Bernard was not given to making cups of cocoa for others, but . . . sleep began to press so heavily on Foran that he retreated to his own bedroom without addressing the problem any further, and slept well into the following day.

Eventually surfacing from unusually deep sleep on the Sunday, Foran organised himself for Mass, was briefed by Bernard to buy a bottle of whiskey for the house while he was out, and provided with money for the purchase. He need not hurry back, Bernard told him.

Next day, it was a different errand that was lined up for

Foran, but it also required him to go a fair distance from the Kirwan house. Scallops or twigs for the thatch that roofed the house were needed, Bernard told him, so he should go to a wood about two miles distant and cut them. Foran mildly pointed out that there were lots of other, more urgent jobs to be done about the farm, but Bernard, rapidly growing into the role of employer, told him to obey orders from the man in charge. Since the man in charge at the time was Bernard, Foran gathered up his tools and set off for the wood, returning only as the dusk was gathering in the late winter afternoon.

On that day, and on almost every day for some time, the gardaí paid a visit to the Kirwan house. Other than his initial slip about his brother being inside the house, Bernard gave no evidence of being flustered. He took calm, considered and appropriate steps as it emerged that Laurence had not gone to visit an aunt in Kildare or anywhere else, but must be thought of as a missing person. At the beginning of December, he despatched a telegram to Radio Éireann (the national radio station which later grew into RTE) giving a description of Laurence and asking that it be broadcast, together with the fact that the man was missing from his home. Radio Éireann consulted the gardaí and then transmitted the message.

Laurence did not respond to the broadcast. Nor did anybody claim to have seen him alive and well. So dragging the Grand Canal was proposed as a method of finding out whether he might have slipped into the waters and drowned. Bernard joined another, married brother and some neighbours two days later as they dragged the canal, which passed close to the family home. Nothing relevant was found. Just after Christmas, the gardaí drained the same stretch of the Canal, but they, too, failed to find anything useful.

Christmas passed, and Bernard had to answer questions from the gardaí every now and again. Sometimes he was helpful, sometimes not. When he was helpful, he gave the investigators hugely detailed accounts of his brother's movements on the night he disappeared. Laurence had stood in front of the mirror doing his hair, wearing a particular pullover (here followed an almost stitch-by-stitch description of the pullover) and with his shirt showing just so much between the pullover and the top of his trousers.

When he was being unhelpful, Bernard would be insolent and brusque. Thus, when asked where he had got the £6 to pay the rates on the Kirwan property, he had got shirty. Even though it was a substantial sum, at the time, for a man with no real income, he told the gardaí that it was his business how he had come by the money and that he would tell them no more than that.

Bernard might have felt powerful in dealing with the forces of the law, but he had managed to break the conditions of his convict's release by going outside the district on one occasion without telling the authorities, and got himself arrested on those grounds. In custody, the gardaí interrogated him again. Perhaps feeling less powerful, but unchanged in his arrogance, he was evasive and abusive.

None of which took the gardaí very much further in their search for the missing man. However, while Bernard was in custody as a result of breaking the conditions of his release, the gardaí did a painstaking search of the Kirwan home. Although bloodstains were found, they were discounted as likely to have been caused during the earlier stabbing incident. More pertinent, decided the investigators, were the clothes they found belonging to the missing man. All over the house were found the kind of items Laurence would normally have worn or carried with him when going out on his bike.

There was the silk scarf. No, friends said. Laurence would never have gone out without it. There was the wallet. No, friends said. Laurence would never have gone out without that. Indeed, said Laurence's girlfriend, he always wore the silk scarf with the overcoat he had been wearing when she had seen him just before he disappeared. On that occasion, he had shown her the wallet and told her he had £70 in it.

Was it a coincidence that Bernard, when arrested, had been carrying just about that amount of money? The gardaí thought this was stretching coincidence just a touch too far, and so as many as fifty of their men were occupied for several days searching the farm, neighbouring farms and bogland around the area in the hope of turning up some clue as to where Laurence's body might be, since they were now under no illusion that he had left his home alive. The investigation was greatly confused by the mistaken testimony of acquaintances who believed they had seen Laurence in Tullamore on some day subsequent to his disappearance. Unless this proved to be inaccurate, Bernard was sitting pretty on an alibi which put him far away from any connection with the disappearance.

The gardaí were not sitting pretty – nor were they sitting still. The systematic and large-scale searches had turned up some pretty interesting circumstantial evidence about Bernard's character. Under his mattress were found newspaper cuttings about sensational murder cases. That wasn't all. Stuffed in the same place was a letter, dating back to his mail robbery, setting out to inveigle a friend to provide him with an alibi. The letter had been sent, and the gardaí had no idea how it had ended up back in Bernard's possession under his mattress, but they figured that a distinguishing factor of the criminal mind is that it tends to repeat patterns of behaviour. Once a criminal's *modus operandi* includes false alibis, they might be expected to recur.

The problem, as the gardaí saw it, was that there was no body. Without a body, proving him guilty of his brother's murder was going to be very difficult. Not necessarily impossible. It had been done before.

In the Ball case (see page 64), Edward Ball had eventually provided the investigating team with a way around the absence of his mother's corpse by telling them she had committed suicide and that he had later disposed of the body. There was no denial of the death or of his involvement in the disposal of the cadaver; the argument in court centred on whether Mrs Ball was a suicide or a murder victim. Similarly, a conviction had been obtained in the case of a young actress who had been murdered on a voyage from South Africa. This girl carried a letter introducing her to the Directors of the Abbey Theatre, and about her death, again, there was no doubt, since the man convicted of her killing admitted that she was not alive, claiming that she had died suddenly and that, panic-stricken, he had squeezed her body through a porthole in mid-voyage.

Laurence Kirwan, however, looked as if he might continue to belong to the "Missing Person" category rather than the "Dead" category, because his brother Bernard was not about to be rattled into any kind of confession as to whether he was among the quick or the dead. Hence, the gardaí had to continue their searches and their collation of the apparently random information they had garnered. One such piece of information was that on the day following Laurence's disappearance, when Bernard had sent Foran far away from the farm to gather twigs for thatching, a neighbour had noted smoke coming from a boiler house on the Kirwan lands. Not only was it going on the Sunday, but it was burning away on the Monday, too, although the boiler, which was metal and had a capacity of fifty gallons, was not in regular use normally.

So the gardaí asked both the workman on the Kirwan lands and his new employer what the significance of the busy boiler was. Foran was mystified, and could recall no use more recent than during the previous spring. Bernard Kirwan, asked the same questions, was evasive.

The State Pathologist now ordered an examination of the boiler house and its contents. Nothing emerged to substantiate the half-formed garda theory that perhaps Bernard had killed Laurence and reduced his corpse to ashes. The theory had been helped along by Bernard's local reputation as a good man to slaughter and bone out a pig, the inference being that he might have done a neat job on the dismemberment and cremation of his brother.

The case was at something of an impasse. Bernard had served the time he had incurred by breaking the conditions of his licence, and had returned to his home, to get on with his life. And pay his bills. One of the bank notes with which he paid a particular debt was identified as having been issued by the bank in Tullamore on the day, just before his disappearance, when Laurence Kirwan had sold his four cows for £50. It was a reasonable assumption that Bernard had now used a bank note which had belonged to his brother just before his brother's assumed death. Interesting, this, but no proof of anything. Particularly with no *corpus delicti.*

The gardaí did more work on the bank note, finding out, by chemical and spectrum analysis that tiny flecks of a rubbery material found on the note had formed part of the lining of Laurence's wallet, which had been found in the house. A little extra pressure could now be put on Bernard by the gardaí, who sought more information about this £70 which had come into his possession around the time of his brother's disappearance. At first, Bernard refused to account for it, but the relentlessness of garda pressure was clearly getting to him, and he tried to persuade a number of friends to tell the gardaí that they had lent him the money. Nobody would agree to this latest scheme, and someone told the gardaí about it, which made them much more confident that Bernard was guilty of murder.

Bernard's lively mind went to work on distractions likely to divert garda interest from him. He made sure that Foran noticed that Laurence's car had a chain on it, to prevent it being driven, apparently intending that Foran would draw the attention of the gardaí to this, and that they, in turn would decide that Laurence, having left his vehicle so protected against use, must be alive and well somewhere and on the verge of returning at any moment. In any case, Bernard claimed, *he* had no idea how to drive the car. Not so, investigation revealed.

Foran, wisely, decided that out of this place he must get, and he abandoned the Kirwan job and house. As the winter wore on, Bernard was on his own. Except, of course, for the regular visitation of gardaí tracking down the latest piece of evidence linking him to the continued absence of his brother.

Bernard did have a social life. Come 17 March, and he, like most Catholics at the time, greeted the one day break in bleak Lent provided by St Patrick's Day with delight, and went to a dance. At which, unfortunately, he lost his coat. Not a bother on him; he was out and about a few weeks later in a different coat. Not a new coat. Just a different coat. A dyed coat. Coloured by Bernard with three packages of black dye he had bought in a shop in Tullamore. The new colour was just to improve the look of the second-hand coat he had bought at a fair in Tullamore, he explained. Off went the gardaí in two directions. One direction was to Dublin, where a cleaning firm lifted the recent dye and established the original colour, allowing a local dressmaker to identify it, from her distinctive stitching, as a coat made by her for Laurence Kirwan. The other direction was to find all of the clothes-stall operators at the local fair. All five of them said they had never sold the coat.

One by one, as winter gave way to spring, the bits of evidence slotted grimly into place. Roughly five weeks after the St Patrick's Day dance at which Bernard had mislaid his own coat, a first cousin of Bernard Kirwan's ran out of hay. The farmer pulled hay from a loft, and in the process uncovered the bicycle on which Laurence Kirwan might have cycled away. It had been missing, and since he had not taken his car, the assumption Bernard would like the gardaí to have adopted was that he had cycled somewhere else. Not so, the bike proved. That was the last day in April.

On the third last day in May, three men went, not to mow a meadow, but to work a bog. Ballincur Bog, at Rahan. The location where they were working was sometimes called Murdering Boreen or Killing Boreen, and there were local tales of ghosts appearing, although some cynics held that these tales, plus the threatening names given to the spot, were designed to deter courting couples.

Because the winter had been very wet, much of the turf they hoped to save as fuel for the following winter was sodden, and this was of more immediate interest to the three men than the fanciful name of the area. It seemed that something was clogging a drain. One of the three went to see what was clogging the drain, taking a fork with him to get rid of the obstruction. The fork stuck in the corner of a sack, and when he lifted the sack he noticed some bones and skin. He called over his employer, and the two sensibly decided to re-bury the remains lest they be interfered with them. The following day, the gardaí were shown the marked site. What had been unearthed was the trunk or torso of a man, packed in sacking. The gardaí now called in the State Pathologist, Dr McGrath, who gave it as his opinion that the trunk was that of "a well-nourished and well-developed man about thirty years of age, which had been buried between six to eight months." At this point, Laurence had been missing for six months.

The torso was taken to Dublin, where an inquest was told that the remains consisted of the chest and backbone of a man. Head, arms, legs and pelvis were missing, as were the internal organs. There was evidence that lime had been used on the skin, that in dismembering the body, a sharp instrument such as a hatchet or a cleaver had been used, and that the operation was "perfect anatomical work." Someone, like a butcher, a vet or a doctor might possibly have done it, but it would have taken a considerable time.

The sack in which the body had been found was called a Blue Seal Binder sack, and had small holes in it. Foran, the workman once employed at the Kirwan farm, was asked about it by the gardaí. Although the identification of a sack might not seem possible, viewed from the perspective of the mass-production nineties or by a city person, not only was this sack familiar to Foran, but he could even tell the gardaí what it had been used for on the Kirwan lands. It had been used to carry tools – hence the many little holes, poked in the sacking by the sharp ends of knives and other implements.

The drain where the torso was found was about a mile from the farm of the two brothers and could easily be reached across the fields. The gardaí decided that they had enough to go on, and before the end of May, they charged Bernard with his brother's murder. Lodging in Portlaoise Prison, Bernard got to work with his pen, writing to a friend seeking an alibi. This letter not only failed to produce the desired alibi, but was eventually used against him in court.

On 18 January, 1943, more than a year after Laurence's disappearance, the case against his brother was opened in Dublin's Central Criminal Court.

The State Counsel told the story of the period of Bernard's imprisonment, during which Laurence, who, like Bernard, had inherited one-eighth of the family farm, kept the place in good order and made money. He went on to the drama of Bernard's return, with its immediate and growing tension for both brothers, and complaints to the workman, Foran, by Bernard, about how his brother didn't want him about the place and wasn't treating him properly. He then suggested that Foran had been drugged by Bernard on the night of Laurence's disappearance. Bernard had some Luminal tablets (barbiturates) which had been prescribed for sleeplessness during his time in prison, and drugging Foran into unconsciousness by doping the cocoa untypically offered to him would have been easy. Foran's heavy sleep would have allowed the prisoner to dispose of the body of the brother he had killed earlier that day.

As the trial progressed, the members of the jury heard that Bernard had saved the Luminal tablets and made no secret of it. In fact, he had written to a girlfriend of his, indicating that if he found she had been dating someone else during his incarceration, he would poison her with them. In addition, they heard how, after Laurence disappeared, a neighbour mentioned to Bernard that the guards had been to her house enquiring about the Kirwans, and had been told by Bernard not to say anything to them. If, asked the State Counsel rhetorically, Bernard had wanted his brother found, would he have given such advice to a neighbour?

Foran, the thirty-five-year-old workman, recounted how he had, shortly after Laurence's disappearance, stopped sleeping at the Kirwan farm, and how Bernard had come looking for him, asking him to come back to work. Not until Laurence returned would he go back, Foran had told him bluntly. "You idiot; the man is all right," Bernard had snapped.

Foran had not been convinced, and left the jury with an impression of Laurence as a man who had been a fair employer and relatively trusting, prior to the return home of his convict brother, at which point he had become paranoid, keeping his money on his person at all times during the daylight hours, and under his pillow at night.

The fifth day of the trial saw an unusual court happening. One of the jurors became seriously ill and a doctor told the judge that the juror was suffering from congestion of the lungs and it was not possible that he could attend the trial for at least a week. The judge decided to continue with eleven jurors, and those jurors soon heard that one of the things Bernard Kirwan had learned to do while in prison was bone pigs. He did this work "in a businesslike way and never made a botch of it" – so if the dead body of Laurence Kirwan had to be sub-divided for eventual disposal, Bernard undoubtedly had the skill to do that in a businesslike way, without making a botch of it.

On the thirteenth day of what was turning out to be a gruelling trial for the remaining eleven jurors, they got their chance to hear Bernard speaking for himself. Stoutly built and dressed in black, he waited for the first question from his counsel.

"You have been charged with slaughtering and butchering your brother," said Mr Ó Briain, SC. "Is that accusation true or false?"

"False in every detail," said the prisoner at the dock, so quietly that both his own counsel and the judge ordered him to speak up.

He did, explaining away the inexplicable sums of money in his possession since Laurence's disappearance as gifts from his now dead mother, entrusted to a female third party to give to him, because he had always been his mother's favourite son. He then went to war against the gardaí, despite the fact that, in his youth, his big ambition was to join their ranks and they had turned him down. Since Laurence's disappearance, he said, they had been shadowing him all over the country. Night, noon and morning. They had made "nuisance raids" on the house.

"That is the only description I can give their visits," he complained. "They were continually coming and looking over the house. They used to come and upset the place, and when it would be set right, they returned and pulled it asunder again. That happened day in, day out."

He doubted the sincerity of the questions they had asked him. They had switched statements he had made and produced in court statements he had never made, and he could tell the difference because he had numbered the pages of the statements he had made.

Tiring of all this, the State Counsel cut through a series of denials on Bernard's part of evidence he had originally given about Laurence dolling himself up in the mirror that Saturday night.

"I suggest to you that that was the last time you saw your brother alive – the time you struck him down from behind."

Silence from the accused.

"Well, what is your reply?" asked the judge.

"I did not think I had to answer such an absurdity," retorted Bernard. "I never struck the man."

In due course, the judge briefed the depleted jury, asking them to leave aside all feelings of indignation, revulsion or horror that they might naturally feel, and to approach consideration of the case with only one purpose in view: the reaching of a just verdict. Seventeen days after the opening of the trial, the jury retired to consider their verdict.

The case had attracted enormous attention, with people queuing for hours outside Green Street Courthouse each morning to pack the gallery and the second jury box, picking and retaining favourite seats for the duration. Many of them travelled from the midlands. Even after the judge concluded his charge to the jury, few people abandoned their hard-won seats, for fear that someone else would take them. The jury retired at lunchtime.

"At 4.10, an official bustle heralded the return of the jury," reported the *Irish Independent*, "and when Kirwan climbed up from the cells hundreds of eyes were focused on him. In front of the dock, a few yards away, sat his sister, Miss M Kirwan. Looking as unperturbed as ever, he took his seat on a cushioned chair in the dock. Here he had sat for seventeen days with a pad of paper on his knees writing continuously and keeping a garda busy carrying written instructions to his solicitor and counsel."

In silence, the court watched Justice M Maguire enter. The verdict was announced. Kirwan was guilty. Justice Maguire donned the black cap and asked Kirwan if he had anything to say as to why sentence should not be passed on him. There was a slight hesitation, and then came the calm, if oratorical, reply.

"At the outset of the case I pleaded not guilty. Throughout the trial I have reiterated my innocence and that is all I have to say. For all the sins of my life I ask forgiveness of God, and ask no forgiveness of man."

Those were not his last words in court. When sentence of death was passed on him, he announced that he forgave his enemies.

Kirwan appealed against his sentence, but the appeal failed, and he was executed on 2 June, 1943.

A NIGHT OF DEBAUCHERY AND A DEAD HONOR BRIGHT

The Ticknock Murder

During the 1920s, respectable Dublin believed that although prostitutes might exist, they certainly did not exist in Ireland's capital city. When O'Casey put Rosie Redmond on the stage of the Abbey Theatre, the audience could not take the representation of a street walker, and, in Yeats's phrase, "disgraced themselves again" by rioting. But fool itself as genteel Dublin might, the reality was out there, and then, as now, the prostitute was a particularly vulnerable person when a male client got murderous.

When the case of Honor Bright came to court, the Counsel for the State clearly wished he was anywhere but in the Central Criminal Court, accusing Dr Patrick Purcell of Blessington, and Leopold J Dillon, a former Superintendent of the Civic Guard (precursors of the Garda Síochána) of murder. Only in the pages of neurotic fiction could you find a tale more disgusting than the tale it was his duty to go through in detail, King's Counsel Mr Carrigan promised. The accused were men of standing. Men of respectability. One was a police officer. A senior police officer. One was a physician, a surgeon, a Peace Commissioner and although a young man, a dispensary doctor in Blessington.

These pillars of the community were charged with the murder of a prostitute. Not that Mr Carrigan, KC, called her a prostitute. She was, he told the court with flowery ambiguity, "an unhappy girl of the unfortunate class." Meaning prostitute. Her name was Lizzie O'Neill. Or rather, that was her name when she was receiving letters. When she was out doing business, she was "Honor Bright". The dead girl, according to Dublin street legend, was in the habit of doing a deal with a customer, and invoking a boy scout-like "honour bright" on the agreement, with the eventual result that the slogan became her street name.

Her death and the court case consequent upon it, had attracted much attention, so that a large crowd assembled outside the courthouse on the first morning of the trial, at the beginning of February 1926. Those who hoped to satisfy prurient instincts were thwarted, however, when it was announced that admission was going to be limited to jurors, witnesses and others who had actual business in the court. When Mr Carrigan rose to make his opening statement, he set out to establish why Dubliners had to be so protected. "It is a hideous tale of a night of debauchery, culminating in the deliberate and cold-blooded murder of one of the unhappy victims of their lust," he announced.

All the villainy, all the debauchery committed by the two accused on that night had been admitted, he added. All of it – except the murder.

Honor Bright had been found at Ticknock Cross on the morning of 9 June 1925. A labourer on his way to work at seven spotted the body, and told the gardaí at Dundrum. The victim was lying on her right side, having been shot dead – instantaneously – by a bullet from a small pistol or revolver. Whoever had shot her had been a marksman. The bullet had gone through her right breast and penetrated both right and left ventricles of the heart before exiting through the left lung. The bullet was found lying under the skin just below the left shoulder blade. A small amount of blood had flowed from her mouth. "Her death was so sudden," said Mr Carrigan, "that her features did not bear the least trace of distortion. She would appear to have risen from the hedge and stepped a foot or two from it when she was shot."

The dead woman had been about twenty-six. Five foot four in height, she was dressed in a grey tweed costume, a mauve crêpe-de-chine blouse, patent shoes, flesh-coloured silk stockings, a black hat and a velvet band in her hair. She had no overcoat. Her pockets held small change, matches and cigarettes and Rosary beads.

The victim, the court was told, was a woman who, through "some cursed necessity" which went unspecified, was forced to seek her livelihood on the streets at night. She lived in Newmarket and had headed out to work at about eleven or half-past on the night of 8 June, together with Madge Hopkins (aka "Bridie") and a few other girls of "the unfortunate class." The girls went about their business, some of them re-convening later on the chains opposite the Shelbourne Hotel, where they sat, chatted, and waited to be picked up.

Dillon and Purcell, who had some business in Dublin that day, had ended up in the Shelbourne Hotel, and were leaving about half-past twelve that night, when they spotted the girls, stopped their car and began to talk to them. Dr Purcell, either furious or drunk, or both, told the girls that he had earlier been with a girl with fair bobbed hair who had robbed him of £11. She would have taken his last quid, he added, if it hadn't been in a separate pocket; the pocket in which he kept his revolver. If he found the said girl, he announced, he was going to do away with her. Those listening to his threats made discouraging noises. Well, he amended, if he couldn't have revenge on her, he would have revenge on somebody else. He then added that his friend, the Superintendent, could blow all of the streetwalkers off the Green if he wished.

Purcell was not just *talking* aggressively. So out of control was he that he was brandishing his revolver. Eventually, he drove off. The sequence of that night's events was difficult to follow in court, but what seems to have happened is that the two men, before midnight, picked up one or more prostitutes, had sex with them, and in the course of the transaction, Dr Purcell was robbed by one of the women, who may or may not have been "Honor Bright."

Having discovered the theft, and probably fuelled his rage with alcohol, Purcell seems to have gone searching for the girl with the fair bobbed hair who had stolen his money, and picked up Honor Bright in the small hours of the morning, possibly for the second time. Between three and four in the morning, a young policeman named Patrick J Burke, stationed at Terenure, was walking his beat on Harold's Cross Road when he saw a two-seater car stopped outside number 3 Waverley Villas. Two men and a woman were standing outside the car. The woman was speaking very loudly, although the policeman could not make out the words. As he moved closer to the trio, they got into the car and drove off in the direction of Terenure, past him.

The policeman later picked Dillon out of an identification parade of a dozen men as one of the two being shouted at by the woman. If the woman was Honor Bright, and if she was the one who had stolen the £11 earlier that night, Purcell and Dillon may have been planning to terrify her into giving the money back. What she hoped to gain from going with them again is moot. It may well have been that the presence of a policeman filled her with fear of arrest, given that either of the two respectable men she was with could have fingered her as soliciting. Whatever the motive, the end result was her death.

Her body, when found, did not look as if she had been killed where she was found. Detectives theorised that she had been shot elsewhere – perhaps in a car – and then dumped.

When the two men were charged with her murder, Dr Purcell said, "I am absolutely innocent," and Dillon went further. "I wish to state that I am not guilty, and I know nothing whatever about this charge." Purcell handed up a gun, which was proven to be incapable of firing the shot which had killed the young woman, although it later emerged that he owned more than one gun.

Testifying in his own defence, the doctor admitted that he and his companion had picked up two girls, one of them known as "Bridie," the other known as "Honor Bright," on the night of the murder. Dillon had gone off with Honor and he had himself gone up Hume Street with Bridie. (Not elaborated in court was the nature of the sexual transaction that ensued, but the timings suggest that neither girl took her "John" to a hotel. A dark corner of a street, or, in Dillon's case, a two-seater car, seems to have been used for fast intercourse.)

All of this, Purcell admitted forthrightly in court, adding

that when he finally reached Blessington about four-thirty in the morning, he had got into his own house through the study window. He was not asked why he had no key. Having gained entrance, he then ate supper and afterwards undressed in his wife's room. His wife made some remark like that it was a nice time to be coming home.

This was a unique outing, he claimed. He and Dillon were not regular customers of the city's prostitutes. He had been doing important police business with Dillon and had gone into the city to have dinner. The yarn about having been robbed was simply bravado, and he could not recall having threatened to do anybody in.

Dillon, following him onto the witness stand, agreed that he had gone off with Honor Bright and had persuaded her to get into the car with him.

A taxi had driven up, he said, "some time later," and Honor Bright had climbed out of the car and got into the taxi, whose driver she seemed to know. The taxi had driven away. Dillon had the impression, he said, that there was someone with grey hair in the back seat of the taxi. But whether there was or there was not a grey-haired stranger in Honor Bright's taxi after she had concluded her business with him, the fact was, he said, that he did not have any quarrel with her that night. Once she left him, he had driven around, picked up the doctor again, and driven home. As they passed a cab, which might or might not have been the same cab into which Honor had climbed, someone had called out "Goodnight."

Dillon had been a second lieutenant in the British army, leaving in 1919 to become a medical student at UCC. Having failed to qualify, he had joined the police force instead. At the time of the murder it was his practice to operate in mufti, and on the night of the murder it had been his plan to have dinner, visit a theatre and go home. Unfortunately, as it turned out, Purcell and he had been too late to get into the theatre.

Dr Purcell's counsel, Joseph O'Connor, KC, protested, when it came to his turn to address the jury, at the way the two men had been demonised by the prosecution. "Is it because they go on a spree and fall victims to the two things that men have fallen victims to from the beginning of time – wine and women – that you are not to judge them by ordinary standards but treat them as human vampires? There is no reason why anyone should so describe these two men who are arraigned before you for their lives."

The point at issue was not whether it was or was not OK to call Purcell and Dillon "human vampires." The point at issue was whether or not they had murdered Honor Bright, but "the unhappy girl of the unfortunate class" seemed to get lost in the prissy shock of the prosecution and the sanctimonious outrage of the defence. It was as if the prosecution were being tried for insulting Purcell and Dillon, not the two men being tried for shooting a young woman dead. In concluding his two-hour-long speech, the defence counsel pulled out every available stop to influence the (inevitably, at that time) all-male jury. "I ask you, gentlemen," he pleaded, "with the greatest confidence, to return a verdict of not guilty against my client (Dr Purcell) so that, with the help of that verdict and the aid of a forgiving wife, he will pick up again those threads of happiness which he has so nearly wrecked through his own folly and win back again, and in due course find himself back in the position he was in when he left Blessington on the evening of 8 June 1925."

Mr Dillon's counsel followed this hearts-and-flowers oration, and not long thereafter, with the prosecution case complete and the judge's summation on board, the jury retired. For all of three minutes. After this phenomenally short consideration, they returned a verdict of "not guilty," and the two men were discharged, to "pick up the threads of happiness" woven through their lives.

Lizzie O'Neill, the prostitute with the cheery pseudonym and the Rosary beads in her pocket, became a half-remembered name in Dublin's oral tradition.

The Man Who Got Away with Murder

A Crime Near Navan, Linked to an Earlier Killing

Nobody heard the shot. Nobody saw the murderer. Nothing but circumstantial evidence linked Joseph McManus to the death of twenty-six-year-old Alice Gerrard. But his odd behaviour – including a suicidal plunge into the floodwaters of the Boyne River – does suggest that McManus may not have wanted to get away with murder. Not this time, anyway. However, there is every reason to suppose that McManus had got away with murder in the early 1920s, almost a quarter of a century earlier . . .

It was a baby's crying that drew attention to the death of Alice Gerrard. The baby was her five-month-old son, and his cries woke his grandmother in the early hours of a Sunday morning. Three generations lived in the three-roomed cottage near Navan. Mary Scott was Alice's mother. She had seen her daughter, Alice, marry Leo Gerrard four years earlier. The marriage was not a success. Leo Gerrard headed for England, while Alice stayed at home and went to work. Four years after they were married, Alice gave birth to a son. Leo Gerrard made it clear that this was no son of his, and that he wasn't going to support him. Alice stayed at home to mind the child, her evenings brightened by more than one male visitor.

When the baby's cries woke Alice's mother early that Sunday morning, Mrs Scott surfaced out of sleep, but stayed in bed for a few minutes, expecting her daughter to comfort the child. For a moment, it sounded as if she had; the cries died down, and in the silence, the grandmother could hear another sound in the cottage. "A sound as of someone walking in stockinged feet," was how she described it.

It was not a frightening sound. Mrs Scott assumed that her daughter was coming down to the kitchen to get a bottle for the baby.

Then came the baby's cry again, and Mrs Scott got up to see what was the matter. She called out to her daughter, but heard no answer.

The cottage had no electricity, so she found her way to her daughter's side by touching the familiar walls and door, guided by the baby's now frantic wails. "Alice? Is there anything wrong?" the older woman asked, reaching out and touching her daughter's face, lifting her head from the pillow. It fell away from her hand lifelessly, leaving the hand wet with blood. The older woman went to get a lamp, and found her daughter slumped in bed, covered in blood, the baby trapped in the crook of her arm. Mrs Scott tried to lift the baby away. It wasn't an easy task. "His legs seemed to be caught under his mother's body as if she fell over him," the grandmother later remembered.

Carrying the baby, Mrs Scott ran to her front door and yelled for help. It was now about a quarter past two. Fortunately, Mrs Scott's next-door neighbour, Miss Rath, hadn't gone to bed until well after half past one, and was a light sleeper anyway, so within minutes of the cry for help, she was up, dressed, and had called in neighbours called

Stapleton. The local priest was called, as were the gardaí and a local doctor.

The arrival of the gardaí stopped the well-meaning tidying of neighbouring women, who, to get the room ready for the priest's visit, had already wiped windowsills and sorted loose debris into cardboard boxes, unintentionally interfering with the scene of the crime and with the crucial details which can help investigators in their work. The arrival of a medical man established what the post-mortem, later in the day, was to confirm: that Alice Gerrard had been shot through the window of her bedroom.

A gun had been poked through the glass at the bottom of the window, Alice had reared up in response to the noise and taken the full blast at close range in the right shoulder and breast area. Severe haemorrhage had caused almost instantaneous death. The baby had been shielded by its mother, but trapped by her collapse. Blood was everywhere, soaking through the mattress and pouring onto the floor.

The immediate reaction in the neighbourhood was that there must be a maniac on the loose. Doors which up to then had merely been latched at night were suddenly locked and barred.

The gardaí, however, were operating on the assumption that most murders are committed by people who are known in the area and who are also known to the dead person. So their searches for the shotgun which had been used to do away with Alice Gerrard quickly turned up a gun in a caravan in which lived a building contractor named Larry Rogers and one of his labourers, Joseph McManus. The gun belonged to Rogers, who had cleaned it only the previous week. When he handed it to the gardaí, however, it was evident that it had recently been used. Suspicion seemed to fall fairly quickly, not on the gun's owner, but on McManus. McManus was known to have had a relationship with Alice Gerrard. He had also mentioned to his friends in recent weeks that he was short of money and falling behind in payments to his estranged wife.

A magnifying glass revealed powdered glass stuck to the rib between the two barrels. Glass from a shattered cottage window? The gardaí went to work on the gun and the window. Who, they asked, had access to the gun? Answer: its owner and McManus. Who had access to the keys which opened the caravan cupboard containing cartridges for the gun? Answer: the owner and McManus, since it was no secret that the keys were kept in Rogers's dungarees.

But the simple answers were not the complete answers. Other people could conceivably have got into the caravan and taken the gun. Other men might have "borrowed" the light dancing shoes also missing from Rogers's property and subsequently found in a field. These shoes matched a footprint outside Alice's window. One of the people who just might have done all of these things was a local farmer known to have been close to Alice.

There was no jumping to conclusions. Just a relentless day by day search of the area, lasting for more than a week. During the same period, McManus was kept under constant observation. The labourer began to show signs of stress. He began to talk too much – always about the Alice Gerrard case. He began to wonder aloud why the gardaí were watching him and what they believed he had done.

He began quite gratuitously to explain away bits of evidence that had already turned up; the mud on a pair of socks found by the gardaí could, he theorised, have been picked up in the yard, rather than anywhere more suspicious. The fact that he was drinking heavily did not help him keep a low profile. It meant that on Monday night, little more than twenty-four hours after the murder, he didn't come back to sleep in the caravan where he lived with his boss. Nor did he go to work. Instead, on the Tuesday, he went to talk to other people in the area, asking them for employment.

"Distracted-looking and very restless," was how one detective described him, forty-eight hours after the murder. He was eager, not to say anxious, to take the gardaí to show them where he had been the previous day. They were less than eager to accompany him on this pointless daytrip.

"I'm not a murderer, anyway," he blurted.

"What put that into your head?" asked one of the surrounding gardaí, all innocence.

"The way you are all coming after me," snapped McManus.

The gardaí mildly responded that they were only inquiring into his movements and making a few notes. McManus subsequently muttered about the "fifth degree," presumably meaning "third degree," the euphemism for physically intimidatory questioning, and told those around him that the gardaí needn't try any of that on him. The gardaí were certainly very suspicious of him by now, but the indications were that he was busily fashioning a noose for himself, and they weren't about to interrupt that process, especially not by engaging in what the Americans call "lockstep surveillance."

(Lockstep surveillance, also known as "rough shadowing" is now illegal in the US, but was used extensively against, among others, the late Sam Giancana. The mobster was pursued by FBI agents who followed him on a twenty-four-hour basis, making no effort to conceal their presence from him or from those around him. Friends of his daughter, for example, were left in no doubt that Giancana père was in dead trouble with the G-men. Fellow golfers were mesmerised when J Edgar Hoover's men, in half-dozen lots, followed Giancana around the golf course and made snide remarks just as he was about to tee off. They even took themselves and their snide remarks (delivered *sotto voce*) into the church when the mafioso went to worship. Eventually, and untypically, Giancana took the Feds to court. Eventually, and untypically, the judiciary found for the mobster, and the FBI were told to lay off what was seen to amount to harassment and infringement of privacy.)

On Friday, when McManus was asked by a neighbour to accompany her on a trip to the shops, he said he couldn't, because the "so-and-sos" (gardaí) were after him. The neighbour wondered aloud if this might possibly have anything to do with Alice's demise? McManus swore at the mention of the dead woman's name. "It's not now she should have been done," he added. "It's long ago."

Six days after the murder, McManus left a local pub at about ten at night, closely watched by the gardaí. When he reached the bridge over the River Boyne, he suddenly climbed it and, in the darkness, plunged into the river.

A garda, Daniel Fitzpatrick, who happened to live near the bridge, was standing at his front door, watching, when

McManus leaped into the flooded river, and he went to his rescue, just failing to grasp McManus as the labourer was swept past him. Now, the gardaí who were following McManus had to turn themselves into a rescue squad. Someone had the bright idea of turning cars around so that their headlights illuminated the river, and the would-be rescuer, Garda Fitzpatrick, was spotted clinging to a branch of an overhanging tree.

Ropes were thrown to him and he was pulled up the face of the river bank. Shortly afterwards, cries for rescue were heard from the opposite bank, and McManus was spotted, "holding on for grim life," one garda said, "to a steep bank against which he had been swept." McManus, too, was dragged on to dry land. "Didn't I tell you I would do away with myself?" he demanded, as they tried to insert his sodden person into a garda car to take him to the station.

At the station, stripped of his wet garments, wrapped in blankets, surrounded by hot water jars and having his pulse taken by a doctor, he changed his mind. "I did not want to drown myself," he announced. "I was nearly gone. Didn't I shout for help?"

Becoming more grandiose, perhaps as the alcohol still in him bolstered his self-esteem, he told his audience (some of them gardaí painstakingly making notes of his every utterance) that he could have swum the Boyne both ways, and that swimming the Liffey would be no bother to him. Sandwiched wetly in among the boasts were obscure denials. "I never did anything to anybody," was one of these imprecise offerings.

When, two days later, he was charged with the murder, his one comment was another denial. "I did not murder her," he said, adding, in vain self-comfort, "I know that myself."

Charged on the fourteenth of one month (October) he found himself in the dock in Green Street on the fourteenth of the following January. In the meantime, much work had been done by the gardaí to firm up the case against him, some of it relating to the double-barrelled shotgun owned by McManus's employer. "We had important evidence from the State Analyst," commented Superintendent George Lawlor, later Chief of the Garda Technical Bureau. "He proved that the fragments of glass found in the gun barrel . . . minute pieces found on McManus's bed and the window glass from Scott's house, were of the same type and similar in composition. Furthermore, he was able to state that the two largest pieces from the gun barrel, the broken glass which had been cleaned up from the floor by the neighbours, and the broken pane still remaining in the window were all of the same thickness – 3.5 millimetres."

There was evidence of a relationship peaking and fading between McManus and Alice Gerrard. At one stage, he had been a regular visitor to her mother's house, playing cards until late at night, and hearing suggestions (or so he claimed) from Alice that he should take his children from their mother and she would take her son and they would all go off together. More recently, however, Alice had clearly gone off the labourer and didn't like him calling to her mother's house. Dislike had an edge of fear, which the young woman had confided to Mrs Scott.

Alice had insisted, in the weeks before the murder, that windows and doors should be secured before she went to bed. She had reckoned without a double-barrelled shotgun poked through the glass of her bedroom window, and an attacker who could kill her with one unheard shot in the dark.

McManus was at pains to portray himself as ignorant of guns and as having never spent time in the army. The gardaí quickly nailed that lie. "During this time, as the result of inquiries which we had made regarding the previous history and employment of Joseph McManus," commented Superintendent Lawlor, "it was established that he had joined the British Army in 1923, at Omagh, and had served in it for a period of twelve years, having been overseas in India from 1924 to 1927."

As the digging into McManus's past went on, it emerged that, almost a quarter of a century earlier, he had been closely involved in another murder. Although this was not referred to during his trial, it raised questions in the minds of the investigators that perhaps they had a man who had not only killed Alice Gerrard, but who had, in the spring of 1923, murdered a girl named Martha Lunny – and got away with it.

Martha Lunny was a quiet, good-looking girl whose family had businesses north and south of the border. They lived in a farm in County Fermanagh, and had a grocery store and public house in Swanlinbar on the southern side. Every day, regular as clockwork, Martha crossed the border on foot, heading for Swanlinbar, where she helped her father in the grocery shop. When the evenings were dark, her sister, who lived in Swanlinbar, would walk with Martha to the border.

On 28 March, the nights were still dark quite early, and so the two girls walked together to the border bridge and there parted company. Martha never made it to her home, and a search the following morning revealed her body in a nearby field, just north of the border.

"An examination of the scene revealed that the unfortunate young lady was first attacked when she was on the road, as signs of a desperate struggle were visible, some of her teeth being found nearby," wrote Superintendent George Lawlor many years after the event. "The body was dragged along the grass margin of the road, through a gate, down a meadow for a distance of over one hundred yards. It was deposited in Northern Ireland within a few yards of the border. A medical examination revealed that the brave girl had died fighting."

Because the girl was found north of the border, the main responsibility for solving the case lay with the Northern police. Longer-established than the newly formed Garda Síochána on the other side of the border, the Northern police nevertheless worked in harmony with the gardaí.

Even though neither force suspected that there was any political implication in the killing, the instability of the times, and rumours that the "Specials" (an RUC force regarded as semi-autonomous in its often grossly violent interpretation of its law-and-order function) had something to do with the Lunny killing, made people uneasy. Understandably, people on the northern side of the border kept their heads down and volunteered little, and were matched in self-protective silence by people on the southern side.

There was one man who was very willing to volunteer information. A young man named Joseph McManus. Living in the North, he said that he happened to be going across the border to the south on the night of the murder, and had met the two Lunny girls. Civil greetings had broken out on all sides, he told the RUC in Kinawley Barracks. On he went. Next he met two men, one in the green uniform of the National Army. This time, according to McManus, uncivil greetings broke out, and the conversation was a tad one-sided, not to say theatrical.

"I have you now," one of the two men told him, ordering him to stand.

McManus, however, had taken to his heels and escaped. However, when far enough away not to fear recapture, he had paused to look back and had seen Martha Lunny pounced on by the two men. "For God's sake don't kill me," was his version of her response to the two men who dragged her off into the meadow under the watchful eye of McManus, who explained his non-intervention by saying he was afraid of being shot. The RUC apparently shared his fear, because they promptly took him into protective custody for six weeks. He told the RUC he would be able to identify the men who murdered Martha, but when a garda superintendent interviewed him he said he wouldn't be able to do it. All he could now remember of the uniformed man was the fact that he had brass buttons on his uniform.

Oddly, in both the Lunny and the Gerrard cases, an evidentiary meddler arrived to muddy the waters. In the Lunny case, an Irish soldier told a member of the gardaí that the man who had done the killing was stationed with the army at Swanlinbar. He later withdrew this claim, saying he had been drunk when he made it. During the Gerrard investigation, a woman presented herself, saying that shortly before the murder, she had been in a car with Alice which had been flagged down by armed and threatening men. The gardaí investigated the alleged incident at great length and eventually satisfied themselves that it was "a mere figment of the imagination." They apparently satisfied McManus's defence on the same point, because the woman was not called to give evidence on his behalf, as it is safe to assume she would have been if the defence believed it might profit their case.

The Lunny case continued to puzzle the gardaí, who believed the murderer was someone who knew Martha's routine and was probably known by her. They sought to have the case moved on – only to find that, not long after he was released from protective custody, McManus had joined the British Army. Now stationed in India, he seemed well out of reach of any further investigation, and so the Martha Lunny case died on the vine, unsolved.

For twenty-three years, that's how it was. Then an ex-British Army man, living away from his wife, started to see a twenty-six-year-old woman living away from her husband, and ended up accused of her murder.

The court case lasted twelve days, and McManus's counsel did not call him to give evidence on his own behalf. Instead, they concentrated on pointing out that the evidence was all circumstantial and could have pointed to any one of several people, not exclusively to McManus. No motive had been proven, said the barrister, Mr Teevan. McManus was completely innocent of the crime, although he had made his suicide attempt "in a state of lunacy." Medical evidence was given by a psychiatrist from Grangegorman, who visited the accused man twice while in prison. The psychiatrist diagnosed the case, according to the reports of the time, as one of "maniac (sic) depression". Other medical men testified to the fact that McManus had at various stages suffered from insomnia and from the visits of non-existent men in his cell. These delusional visitors were sometimes very tall, and sometimes very small.

Since they were not claiming that McManus had murdered Alice Gerrard while insane, but rather claiming that he hadn't murdered her at all, his counsel had to acknowledge that, as they put it, "McManus was a happy-go-lucky type, unstable and a moody fellow who danced jigs in the public street and who might not speak to his best friend the next day," while trying to convince the jury that this did not add up to a murderous profile.

Despite their best efforts, and possibly helped by some pointed questions posed by the judge in his summing-up, the jury took little more than four hours to find him guilty and bring in the verdict with a recommendation to mercy. The judge asked McManus if he had anything to say. There was a long hesitation, and then he thanked politely the judge who had just sentenced him, the jury who had just found him guilty, and "Mr Teevan and Mr de Valera for the grand defence they put up for me."

Leave to appeal was denied on 14 March, and McManus was executed on the final day of that month – hanged by Pierrepoint, the British hangman. (See page 50)

The gardaí who investigated the Alice Gerrard case could not but ask themselves if McManus had perhaps escaped justice twenty-three years earlier. "On his own admission, he was present when Martha Lunny was killed and many people were convinced that he was the murderer," commented Superintendent Lawlor. "In each case, a defenceless female was done to death, at night, by a killer who left the public roads and went panther-like through the fields after his prey . . . "

DARKNESS VISIBLE

The Body at the Bottom of Falmore Quarry

The setting could have been lifted out of a pot-boiler Abbey Theatre play during the 1940s. Here we have this quiet country curate named Fr James McKeown, serving in a small village near Dundalk in Co. Louth. The quiet curate has a housekeeper, who is thirty-six and single. The quiet curate also has a handyman who doubles as a driver for him.

As spring was turning into summer in 1927, all this orderly rural living went slightly wrong. The housekeeper went missing. In the beginning, it would have been leaping to conclusions to say that she had gone missing. It was just that Fr McKeown's supper wasn't left ready for him one evening where Mary Callan, the housekeeper, would normally have left it. The fire had been let go out, too. Fr McKeown decided to head for bed, puzzled that his normally reliable housekeeper should have done an unexpected flit on her bike without leaving him even the briefest message.

Fr McKeown didn't alert the gardaí at this point, although he did a small investigation of his own, which showed that Mary's best hat and coat were missing from her wardrobe. The priest had to get to bed in order to get up to say Mass the following morning.

Morning came. Mass was said. Back came Fr McKeown to his house, and there was no sign of the missing Mary. So Fr McKeown pressed the young handyman into service. Would he light the fire? He would. Would he please make the breakfast? Definitely. And organise hot water? Certainly. As Gerard Toal, the teenage handyman, was setting about these tasks, the priest asked him what he knew about Mary's movements the day before.

Mary had been encountered by Toal, the housekeeper dressed in the best coat and hat which were gone from the wardrobe, some time early the previous afternoon. She was going away for good, she had told him.

Flummoxed wouldn't now come near to summarising Fr McKeown's frame of mind. Women in Ireland in the twenties did not up stakes and abandon jobs that easily. Nor did they tend to abandon their home place and all of its contents without a backward glance – yet there was no evidence that the housekeeper had as much as packed a bag.

Fr McKeown went to have a look at Mary's room, to see what she might have taken with her, although logic dictated that whatever she had taken must have been small enough to fit in an overcoat pocket. Her suitcase? There. Her books? In position.

Her family photographs? All lined up, facing into the empty room. Her Bible? Present.

Her Rosary beads? Clustered on a shelf, ready for a reaching hand.

A successful career woman in her late thirties at the present time might grab her credit cards, abandon the detritus of a past life, and head for Europe or the US.

But in the 1920s, a priest's housekeeper who was a single woman given to prayer and solitude was unlikely to leave behind her every precious possession, and head into the wide blue yonder on a bicycle without giving notice to her employer or confiding in anybody other than a teenage handyman. Sense it did not make.

Mary's employer decided to locate Mary's mother to see if she could throw light on the disappearance of her daughter. He asked Gerard Toal to drive his old black Ford car to where the mother lived, roughly thirty miles away, and make enquiries there. Off went young Gerard.

Came the afternoon, and back came young Gerard, without much light to throw on the subject. Mary's mother was as mystified as was Fr McKeown by her disappearance, and indicated that if Mary had disappeared, she hadn't disappeared in a homeward direction. Gerard Toal delivered all of this less-than-helpful information and added a rider. Mary Callan had something wrong with her, he suggested, and this was why she had gone away.

This comment seems to have fallen like a feather into the Grand Canyon. Nobody pursued it.

The following day, Fr McKeown decided that this situation needed outside help, and so he called in to his nearest garda station and told the whole story to the gardaí. The gardaí voiced the comment which police forces worldwide tend to voice in such circumstances: two or three days isn't a long time to be missing – wasn't it a little early to be thinking suspicious thoughts about Mary's fate?

Fr McKeown went home to think it over and as the third week of May began with Mary now missing for about four days, he went back to the gardaí to put it on record that this was untypical behaviour on the part of his housekeeper and that he was worried sick about her. When no investigation ensued, he went, on 30 May, to the much bigger garda station in Dundalk and demanded action. He got it.

Two gardaí appeared. Interviewees (including the priest himself) were lined up and questioned. Nobody actually yelled "Book him, Danno," but there was expectation that something would happen. It didn't.

The Mary Callan case seemed to be distinguished by its capacity to come to the boil and drop back to lukewarm temperatures within a matter of minutes. When the two investigators were around, it was at boiling point. After they had gone, it was back to lukewarm, and a promised visit by a more senior officer never happened.

When a month had passed since Mary's disappearance without knock, beck, wreathed smile, letter, telegram, postcard or phone call, the priest began to get as close to agitated as a quiet country pastor ever gets. Mary's wages were ready for her, neatly made up as they normally would be. Fr McKeown put them in a drawer and tried to get on with his work. The church sent him on a two-month course that summer – maybe when he came back Mary would have arrived or sent a letter explaining her uncharacteristic absence.

She didn't.

Summer moved into autumn, and Fr McKeown walked his small grounds, pondering the problem. Stables at the back of the house not only held his pony and trap, but also the black Ford that Gerard had driven when seeking information from Mrs Callan. Above the stables was a loft, where Gerard slept.

Suddenly desperately needing to find information, any

information, to help him solve the mystery, the ageing priest climbed into the loft room and looked around. Incurious by nature and given to respecting the privacy of his employees, he had never been in Toal's room before. A discrepancy met his eye immediately. Shoved into a makeshift shelf over the bed was a blanket. But it wasn't Toal's blanket. It was Mary Callan's. The priest showed it to the woman who was filling in for Mary as his housekeeper. Her name was Peggy Gallagher, and she was a pal of Mary. She readily confirmed his judgement; it definitely was Mary's blanket.

Toal was asked to explain. Denial broke out. It wasn't Mary's blanket at all. It was his. He'd had it for ages and ages. Honestly. Honestly?

Not in Peggy Gallagher's view. Peggy now had the investigative bit between her teeth, and she pushed her employer to have another look in Toal's room. Almost a year after Mary Callan's disappearance, he did, finding, oddly, several pieces of a disassembled lady's bicycle. Not only were they present in Toal's room, but they were beautifully cleaned.

At first glance, the saving and cleaning up of bicycle parts by a teenager with a knack for fixing things would not seem to be a pointer towards criminal activity, but the priest had, in fact, happened upon a vital clue. He also discovered a lady's watch which had been tinkered with. Peggy Gallagher was sure that this had been Mary Callan's watch.

Suppertime came, and Gerard Toal arrived for his meal, to be faced by his employer, asking questions about the bicycle parts. As always, Gerard had a ready explanation. He was, he said, something of a buyer and seller of old bicycle parts, dealing regularly with repair shops.

The priest did not believe him. The bicycle parts looked to him as if they had been cannibalised from Mary Callan's bike. No, no, no, Toal said. These bike parts had been purchased here, there and yon in order to make up a new bicycle, and if he couldn't achieve that, he could always sell them again. Simple as that. Indeed, now that he thought about it, hadn't he bought one bit – that very bit there – from a man named Tom Halfpenny up in Blackrock.

Suddenly, the priest, who had, up to now, accepted explanations and tolerated procrastination, became relentlessly pursuant. He ordered the teenager into the car to drive him the ten miles to Halfpenny's house. Cleverly, when he got there, he ordered the handyman to stay in the car, and went into the house on his own. Could he talk to Thomas Halfpenny, he asked the woman of the house. Well, no, he couldn't, came the civil answer. Her son didn't live at home any more. OK, where did he live? America. America? Yes. Since when?

Since he emigrated. When did he emigrate? Thirteen months before.

Back to the car went McKeown and ordered the young driver to take him to the big garda station at Dundalk. As they drove, the priest tersely told the young man that he no longer believed any of his stories, and that his claim to have recently bought a bicycle part from Tom Halfpenny was blither, since the "seller" hadn't been in the country for more than a year.

There was a long silence. Toal obviously figured that denial would not do. If he was to be believed in this tight situation, he had to come up with something which was more interesting to the priest than the theory inevitably forming in the priest's mind. "Father, I'll tell you the truth," he blurted. "I broke into Williamson's bicycle shop in Dundalk and I stole the parts."

The priest looked straight ahead. This new offering put the label of "thief" on Toal, as well as pre-existing labels of "liar" and "possible murderer". On arrival at Dundalk Garda Station, the priest frog-marched Toal in, told the gardaí the Williamson's shop story, and sat down to await the results of their investigation. It proved to be brief. In picking Halfpenny as the seller of the bicycle part, Toal had been unfortunate, because Halfpenny hadn't been in the country at the time the alleged transaction had taken place. In picking Williamson's as the shop from which he had supposedly nicked the bike part the priest now knew he hadn't bought from Halfpenny, Toal pulled a dud, too.

The shop hadn't been broken into in living memory and nothing was missing. Were they sure? Of course they were sure. Would they mind if a garda went around to check their locks? Not at all. He'd be welcome.

The Halfpenny story was dead. Now the Williamson story was dead too. Not dead was Gerard Toal's endless self-exculpatory creativity, which allowed him, on the run, to develop a new scenario, which had a self-confessed thief, in a wild panic, thrusting the bike parts into Toal's hands and making him promise that he (Toal) would never reveal the name of the thief to anyone.

The gardaí went back to the priest's house to have a look. Remember the lady's wrist-watch? Fr McKeown did. But the gardaí didn't find it. Where was it, they asked Toal, who took it out of his jacket pocket, where he had hidden it at the beginning of the search. Why had he hidden it? No reason, really, he said. He had bought it for sixpence. From what seller? Halfpenny, perhaps? Unfazed, Toal said he did not know the man who had sold it to him.

The gardaí went away to consider all this, leaving Toal where he was. Fr McKeown sat down to consider all this, and decided that he could not leave Toal where he was. He fired him. Toal took his dismissal well, allowing as how he might head for Canada. Wonderful, thought the priest, and drove him to Belfast. Nice knowing you. Safe journey. Bye, Bye . . .

Forty-eight hours later, Toal was making like the proverbial bad penny. He was back. Why was he back? Well, there was this small problem, you see. He had stayed with a relative in Belfast, because the next ship to Canada wasn't due for a few days. During those few days, the gardaí had caught up with him. No, not about Mary Callan. About the good suit he was wearing, which seemed to have a resemblance to a suit stolen from a draper's shop in Dundalk, where there had been a break-in just before Toal had gone north. The young man was brought south, questioned about the suit and charged with its theft. Almost as an afterthought, the gardaí lobbed a few questions at him about the bicycle parts.

Like Scheherazade, Toal, to keep himself ahead of the posse, crafted a new story, which was a variation on the Williamson's shop edition, but which does not merit repetition here.

A year after Mary Callan disappeared, a Garda Superintendent led a large party of officers out to Fr McKeown's house where, for the first time, they did an exhaustive search of the premises and of the grounds, turning up various bits and pieces, several of the latter belonging to a lady's bicycle. In addition, there were bits of a woman's handbag, partly burned clothing (female) and a section of a blanket. The findings were made just about everywhere. Some were located under a refuse heap, some were found when digging was done on recently disturbed soil. Toal's response to the whole array of the findings was a sustained shrug and a claim that he had never seen, owned, touched or made the acquaintance of any of them in his life.

It may have taken the gardaí a year to get serious about Mary Callan's disappearance, but serious they now were. The Superintendent questioned Toal at great and unsatisfactory length, and then went for a long walk in the area surrounding the priest's house, to think it all over. The things Toal was saying – indeed, as the Superintendent was now hearing – the things Toal had been saying from the very day of Mary's disappearance, was at best inconsistent and at worst, downright suspicious.

The Superintendent's wanderings took him about five hundred yards from the priest's house, through a little wood and to a point where he could lean on a fence and look down, forty feet, into the waters of a quarry. Falmore Quarry was an impressive sight, large, oblong, with sheer sides and a central depth of almost fifty feet. Darkness visible. Darkness in the depth of the waters, darkness in the surround of tall trees.

The senior policeman added a year of unfinished business together in his head and made a courageous decision, based on speculation. The speculation was that Mary Callan had been murdered and that her body was probably at the bottom of Falmore Quarry. The decision was to ring Garda HQ in Dublin to seek authorisation to drain the quarry quickly. Garda HQ agreed to the request, and off went the heavies of the Dublin Fire Brigade to pump out the millions of gallons of dark water sitting in the quarry. It took them four days to get near the bottom, but as soon as they did, one of the firemen pointed. There was something sitting on the muddy bottom of the quarry, and it looked like a large sack. They got near enough to snag the fabric with a spade and drag it to dry land.

The Superintendent, who must have been fearful that nothing would be found, having watched the intensive pumping of this huge body of water for almost a week, took it upon himself to cut the sack open. The seeping, decomposed horror of the contents proved his speculation to have been well-founded. The sack contained the rotted, long-immersed body of a woman. It was stark naked, and the head and legs had been cut from the rest of the body.

Two forensic pathologists went to work on the body and, within a matter of days, what was emerging was that it was yielding up a great deal of information, but that not all of it would help prove a charge of murder. The body had been so long in the cold waters of the quarry that signs which might have pointed to the precise cause of death were no longer present. The hyoid bone was broken, which might indicate a thump to the neck or attempted strangulation, but it might indicate a number of other possibilities, too. Mary Callan was not pregnant when she died, and her dead body showed no evidence of a disease that might have caused her death.

What the dead body did show, however, was that whoever had cut her head and her legs away from her body in the attempt to make the whole corpse fit more easily into the hessian sack, had known something about anatomy. The two pathologists were not suggesting that whoever had dismembered Mary had been a surgeon. On the contrary, the kind of rudimentary skill shown might be gained by someone who had, at some stage, worked as a butcher. The gardaí grimly added this fact to their file, knowing, as they did, that Fr McKeown had taken Toal on as a handyman after he'd been fired from a junior post in a butcher's shop.

There was never much doubt that the corpse was that of Mary Callan. Although she was naked, whoever had dumped her in the quarry had stuffed her clothing into the sack along with her, and these items were speedily recognised as having belonged to the priest's housekeeper. Her false teeth, also present, were identified by her dentist.

But the big sodden sack yielded up one more critical piece of data, this time unrelated to Mary, but linking someone else to the disposal of her body. The big cloth bag had been secured at the top with a strip of cloth. That strip of cloth was later proved to have come from a man's shirt. The shirt was owned by Gerard Toal.

At the beginning of June 1928, Gerard Toal was charged with the murder of Mary Callan, and not much more than a month later, he was fighting for his life in court.

During the court case, the flak flew in all directions. Fr McKeown was described by one of the barristers, acting for the State, as "credulous," because, he pointed out, the priest "had searched everywhere except the one place where there was a veritable mine of information – Toal's room. You would think that the powers of darkness had darkened Fr McKeown's understanding," the barrister scoffed. Which seemed just a little hard on a priest who had done as much informal investigating as most employers would have done, and who had made at least five visits to different garda stations to try to get the official investigators interested in the missing person status of his housekeeper. Although the barrister did, later, apologise, it was a humiliation for the old priest.

Peggy Gallagher, the dead woman's friend, on the other hand, could not have been described as "credulous." She had unofficially searched Toal's room more than once and found all sorts of items in it which self-evidently didn't belong to him, including Mary Callan's missal with her name rubbed out in a botched way and Gerard Toal's substituted.

If there had been ban-ghardaí around at the time, working in the Special Branch, Peggy Gallagher would have been a cert, not just for a career, but for fast promotion. Not only had she refused to buy any of Toal's creative anecdotage, but she had refused to go along with Fr McKeown's gentle respect for privacy, and had searched the hell out of Toal's room in his absence, making sense of what she found there. In addition, she made a startlingly significant find outside the priest's house, where she spotted, stuck in a hedge running between the garden and a field, a piece of sacking. Over she went and yanked it off the branch to which it was adhering. Not only was it sacking, she decided, it was familiar sacking. It looked amazingly like the sacking in the big bag that had contained Mary Callan's dismembered person at the bottom of the nearby quarry.

Peggy Gallagher took her finding to the gardaí, who treated it with respect, possibly because they would by now have realised that this lady was no dozer. Out came the sack, and sure enough, it had a hole in it. The piece of sacking pulled out of the hedge matched that hole so precisely that no doubt was left; the two had once been one. The gardaí now faced the likelihood that the murderer had pushed Mary's body into the sack and set off by the quickest route to the quarry.

The quickest, most direct route meant going through a gap in the hedge. Since the gap was not quite large enough to accommodate sack, contents and carrier, it had been a struggle to get through, and a prong of hedge had plucked away a section of the sacking.

The barrister for the state might have rather harshly jeered at the priest for his credulity, and have had to apologise later for this onslaught, but his problems were in the halfpenny place compared to the difficulties facing counsel for the defence. They might have, through gritted teeth, repeated to each other the Victorian adage to the effect that: "O, what a tangled web we weave/When first we practice to deceive . . . "

Because Gerald Toal had woven a tangled web of creative lies, many of them pointless. The nineteen-year-old seems to have been incapable of learning from his past disasters, because, in the box, he piled on more and more lies, variations and embroideries, all of them pointless and most of them actively counterproductive. At one point, he was asked, in an effort to get to the truth of the Williamson's shop story, how he had got into that shop, given that the shop owners and staff said that there had never been a break-in, never a smashed window, never a jimmied lock.

Toal took a deep breath and came up with the answer. He had tried Fr McKeown's house keys, he averred, and they had just happened to fit the door. The jury was left to believe that Toal was a serendipitous thief who set out to steal on the off-chance that the borrowed keys of his employer might fit the door of his victim.

Not that Toal abandoned earlier stories. Some of them he stuck with, even though his barristers must have told him that they were likely to take him straight into the hangman's noose. One of the stories he opted to be faithful to was the story that he had bought the lady's wristwatch from a total stranger. Another was his tale of a conversation with Mary in which she had told him she was going away forever.

Four days after the trial began, it ended with the judge's summing up. The jury retired at nine o'clock at night. The courtroom did not clear – there was a deadly sense that the jury's task, although not easy, might be very simple, and so people assumed it would not be an all-night deliberation. They weren't, however, expecting the jury to return not much more than half an hour later. The stir the return caused died down; the jury just wanted to ask the judge a technical question. Back they went to the jury room. Fifteen minutes later, however, they came back again. This time, it was with a verdict. Guilty. The judge then asked Toal if he wanted to say something.

"I am not guilty, My Lord," the teenager said.

There was a pause, and he tried to speak again. This time, the terror of his situation overcame him, and no understandable words came out of the white-faced youngster. The judge sentenced him to death.

If Toal had been overcome just before sentence, he regained his composure completely in the weeks following, during which an appeal was unsuccessfully made, and a petition, also unsuccessful, sent to government for a reprieve. In prison in the few weeks leading up to his execution, he seemed without either remorse or concern over the death of Mary Callan.

But then, given that he seems to have committed a strangely trivial and passionless murder, it was perhaps congruent that his response to his own death would have been trivial and passionless. Toal was never suspected of murdering Mary Callan for the £120 she had in a local bank, even though this was a substantial sum at the time and represented the spinster's life savings. No. It was a murder for bicycle parts, which he had planned to disassemble and sell. To that end, a woman in her thirties had been killed, dismembered and left to decompose in the depths of the waters of Falmore Quarry, while her murderer had appropriated her missal and scribbled his own name on it . . .

Gerard Toal died at the hands of the executioner on 19 August 1928.

INCONTINENTLY PACKED ACROSS THE OCEAN – TO KILL

Murder by a Post-Famine Emigrant

Ireland has always exported people. It has never put such a crude term on the process, of course. In the Dark Ages, our sending out of scholars and missionaries was seen as the bringing of enlightenment to parts of Europe. In the nineteenth century, we supplied the infrastructural human resources of the industrial revolution – the navvies and the gangers on the building sites and the railways. In the earlier parts of this century, we exported writers who could not stand the constraints of the Irish mindset, not to mention the horrors of the Irish censorship system. In the last couple of decades, we have exported our best and brightest to work in the sunrise industries of Europe and America.

Not much attention has been given to the fact that we've also done a brisk export trade in murderers, down through the years, although a recent book (Sean O'Brien, *Bloody Ambassadors*) redressed the balance somewhat. As its author points out, " . . . as murderers, the Irish exiles hold their own with the very worst." Not only have we exported murderers, but we have exported a fair number of *female* murderers. Women like Charlotte Bryant and

Kate Webster have figured in crime anthologies for decades.

Less well known is the case of Bridget Durgan, who never got noticed by anybody until she was accused of murder. Bridget, in her teens, was just one of the increasing number of women leaving Ireland. This increase, according to historian Kerby Miller, was due, at least in part, to the low status of *mná na hÉireann* at the time.

"One index of Irishwomen's deteriorating status," he says, "was a great increase in female emigration: between 1856 and 1921 about half the Irish emigrants were women, and from Connaught and west Munster – where farm life was especially harsh and non-farm employment practically non-existent – females constituted a majority of the exodus." (Kerby A Miller, *Exiles and Emigrants*.)

James Connolly was later to write about these women that: "Laws made by men shut them out of all hope of inheritance in their native land; their male relatives exploited their labour and returned them never a penny as reward, and finally, when at last their labour could not wring sufficient from the meagre soil to satisfy the exertions of all, these girls were incontinently packed across the ocean . . . "

Bridget Durgan was so "incontinently packed across the ocean" from her home in Sligo to the US that she could never remember in which year she had made the journey. Like the rest of the women who made that journey, she had been fed promises of a freer, better life. Like most of them, she was, in reality, headed for domestic service at best and for little more than slavery at worst. Emigrants of both sexes in the years after the Famine found themselves at the bottom of the ladder, competing in the north with free Negroes, in the south with slaves, and often working in grim, even dangerous conditions for miserable money.

The conditions in which Bridget worked were not the worst, but she seems to have had little security, spending no more than a few months in most positions before moving on.

However, when she reached her early twenties, her luck changed. In late October 1866, she went to work for Mrs William Coriell. Coriell was a doctor in his forties, married to a woman ten years his junior. The couple had only one living child, a two-year-old daughter, because Mrs Coriell was frail and had miscarried many times.

All of Bridget Durgan's Christmases seemed to have come together. Here was a family that showed her kindness and treated her well, even approved of her, because Coriell was heard to say that the Irish girl was quiet and peaceable and that she treated his wife with respect. She was earning eight dollars a month, and for almost four months, those eight dollars changed hands without difficulty.

It was in February that frail little Mary Ellen Coriell lit one end of a long fuse that was to blow her into eternity not long afterwards. She discovered that Bridget had "filthy" habits. Just what these were has never emerged, but whatever they were, Mary Ellen wasn't having them in her house, and she gave her notice.

As Bridget moved about the house during the days before she left, washing her own and the family's clothing, she was desolate, telling friends that she didn't think she would ever get as good a position with such kind people as the doctor and his (now enraged) wife. A look out of the Coriell's window would have exacerbated her misery.

It was snowing, the drifts of white giving a chilling indication of what it was going to be like to be out on the streets a few days later.

Dr Coriell, who had never had much of a problem with Bridget (although, as it later emerged, the servant girl had presented the family with challenges quite outside of her non-specific "filthy habits") went off in the afternoon of Monday 25 February 1867, to deliver a baby, his last picture of the Irish girl one of domestic business as she ironed her skirts.

In the middle of that night, with Dr Coriell still away at the birthing, Bridget suddenly appeared at the house of an elderly cousin of the doctor, clutching the Coriell's two-year-old in her arms, her hair and clothing in complete disarray, yelling about burglars in her place of work. The elderly relative panicked and refused to let her in.

Bridget ran on in her stockinged feet through the snow and the darkness to the home of the clergyman, who opened his door and let her in, noting that she didn't even have a skirt on over her petticoat. The Minister half-listened to Bridget's wild ramblings about two burglars who might, she assured him, at that very moment be upstairs in the Coriell's home, murdering Mary Ellen. Knowing that Bridget was not very bright, the Minister made the assumption that someone had made a late call to the doctor's home seeking his help, and that Bridget, because she had been heavily asleep, had added two and two together and made it into six. The clergyman's main concern was that a two-year-old had been dragged through inclement night weather and might take a chill.

The Minister and his wife took care of the child and

listened to Bridget's story, lighting lamps and finding a gun at the same time. The lighting of the lamp revealed a big splotch of blood on Bridget's petticoat, which she promptly sat on, thereby concealing it from view.

The Minister, booted, unlike Bridget, made the journey to the Coriell's house, which he found in considerable disorder, with overturned and broken chairs in the sitting-room, floating feathers everywhere, apparently released from a damaged bed, and smoke, rather than flames, coming from the same bed.

At this point, several neighbours had joined the clergyman in the Coriell home, and the bed was swiftly drenched with water to stop it bursting into flames. That, however, turned out to be the least of the neighbours' worries, for the house also contained the brutalised body of Mary Ellen Coriell. It had not been an easy death, nor had it been a passive one. Since the swelling and bruising which showed all over the tiny woman's body could not have happened after death, both showed that she had fought hard for her life. Her face was swollen and discoloured by bruising, and there were just under thirty cuts and slashes on her neck and body. One of the most gruesome wounds was to her right hand, where she seemed, in desperation, to have grabbed the blade of the knife which had been used to slash her, and cut herself to the bone in the process.

More than a knife had been used. Mary Ellen's diminutive body showed teeth marks and the evidence that someone had torn clumps of her hair out of her scalp. Who could have done such a thing to the doctor's wife?

Bridget had the answer. Two men had done it. When? Eight thirty that night. Or it might have been seven thirty.

In fact, that was when they had come looking for the doctor, but later they had come back and asked for him again. Who let them in? Mrs Coriell, came the quick answer. Or maybe it was Bridget herself, on Mrs Coriell's instructions. What did they look like? One was tall, one was short. One was blond, one was dark-haired. One was clean-shaven, one had a moustache. Would Bridget recognise them again? That produced a tripartite answer: No. Maybe one of them. Maybe yes to both of them.

When the doctor came home, he began to poke holes in Bridget's story. She claimed that his wife, at the men's first visit, had told them the name of the town where Dr Coriell was assisting the birth. That, the Doctor believed, was not in character. His wife was much more likely, if the visitors had an urgent need of him, to direct them to the precise house he was attending. The doctor was also influenced in his thinking by the gruesome bite marks on his wife's body. Received wisdom at the time held that only women bit people. Therefore a woman had killed Mary Ellen. The nearest woman with a handy grudge was Bridget, so maybe the murderer was not male, blond nor moustached, but a female in her early twenties with an Irish accent . . .

As doubts were forming in the doctor's mind, circumstantial evidence was helping them set into concrete conviction. The circumstantial evidence included Bridget's bloodstained petticoat, which she speedily washed, a meat-slicing knife from the kitchen, bent out of shape, which was discovered the day after the murder in a garden shed following a visit there by Bridget, and the lack of any footprints in the snow to support her story of the two male attackers.

It did not help Bridget's case that her sense of timing was not very precise. She claimed that she had run for help the moment the attack started, and that the attack had started the moment the attackers arrived in the house, which was at about half past ten, yet she had not turned up at the door of the clergyman's house, a hundred yards away, until well after midnight. Nor was it helpful that the doctors examining the corpse estimated that Mrs Coriell had fought for at least one hour and probably longer. It was inevitable that the question should be asked: where was Bridget during all of this murder and mayhem?

She was quickly charged with the murder of her former employer, and, just as quickly, details of her former life seeped out, whether accidentally or deliberately, which cast doubt on the picture of mutual satisfaction she had painted. Mrs Coriell, it was now said, had, long before the revelation of the "filthy habits," been dissatisfied with the level of neatness presented by Bridget. Nor was she at ease with the problems posed each month by Bridget's period. And the Irish girl's "fits." These were diagnosed by the doctor as cataleptic seizures close to epilepsy. When they happened, Bridget would suddenly become very drowsy, then go rigid, staring at nothing, occasionally rocked by muscle spasms. When the "fit" finished, Bridget would often sleep heavily for an hour or so. When these happened, the doctor had to hire another woman to look after Bridget, and the arrangement was becoming unsatisfactory and costly.

After her arrest, Bridget continued to have these attacks in prison, observed by her jailers.

"Sitting on a box she would fall off, be senseless a few moments, then open her eyes, and then sometimes say her head pained and sometimes that she felt well," one of those jailers said. Others talked of her frothing and producing blood from her mouth as a result of biting her tongue. But always, they reported, she eventually got over these fits and went back to her normal sleepy look.

Even that sleepy look put most visitors off her. Bridget was to learn a heartless truth: that those who most often claim to be concerned about individuals and to seek to come to terms with the essence of a person rather than their appearance, in fact make judgements based on appearance which they later rationalise into broader-based judgements of character. Visitors, some of them eminent in their fields, visited the Irish girl in prison. From the accounts they left of their visits, it is fair to infer that they visited out of a desire to observe, rather than a desire to succour or understand. One after another, they came away from their encounters with this illiterate and inarticulate woman, with pejorative accounts of her "heavy," or "large, coarse" person. They talked of her cat-like teeth, her eye like "the eye of a reptile in shape and expression" and of her resemblance to "many inferior animals." Class hatred, racism and sexism came together to find Bridget Durgan not just guilty until proven innocent, but of a different and lower species of humanity than her victim.

At the very beginning of her trial, the *New York Times* reported that "the guilt of the accused seems to be a foregone conclusion among outsiders and when the counsel for the prosecution makes a good point there is a sympathetic buzz and flutter throughout the courtroom." This, despite the fact that Bridget's lawyer had first of all warned the jury against the "prejudice in this community" and asked them not to be influenced by it.

Apart from this plea, the defence was undistinguished. It amounted to an attempted point-by-point rebuttal, and it failed. A defence attorney outlining his client's side of a story and then announcing that the state's case adds up to "nothing" may make for a strong assertion but it can be seen through by a jury.

To cover themselves, the defence team also half-depicted Bridget as mad. If she did what she claimed, they said, she must be either innocent or mad. Run though the snow with blood on her petticoat? Only an innocent or a lunatic would have done it. Identify by name (as she briefly did) two men who could be checked as having alibis? Only an innocent or a lunatic would have done it.

If the defence had been less "innocent" themselves, they might have opted to suggest that Bridget, far from being innocent, was guilty but insane, but having outlined the possibility of insanity, they backed away from it. Leading criminologist, Ann Jones, examining the case in 1979, came down firmly on the side of Bridget as a sick woman of very low intelligence.

"It seems clear in retrospect," Jones wrote, "that she suffered from frequent, severe *grand mal* epileptic seizures, and that she probably killed Mary Ellen Coriell while suffering what modern medicine calls a seizure of psychomotor or temporal lobe epilepsy – a type of seizure often characterised by rage, physical violence and amnesia. Even at the time her attorneys might have entered on her behalf a plea that reflected her diminished responsibility – a plea of not guilty by reason of insanity, or guilty of a lesser charge of homicide or manslaughter – for medical jurisprudence already knew something of epilepsy."

One of the factors telling *against* Bridget in relation to

this possible plea of insanity was that she had been treated by Dr Coriell himself for whatever ailed her, and he, in his testimony to the court, was not going to allow it to be believed a) that he had failed to control what was wrong with her, and b) that she was not really guilty of the appalling slaying of his frail wife because she was insane. She had fits, Dr Coriell agreed, but she was sane.

If the man who had been markedly kind to her in the past contributed, in court, to her downfall, Bridget was also poorly served by the judge, who does not seem to have bothered even to pretend to have a dispassionate approach. On the contrary, perhaps fearing that, although Bridget's appearance was far from seductive, her gender might provoke sympathy from the jury, he moved to head the possibility off at the pass by explaining to them that Bridget had "unsexed herself" by the crime and could, therefore, claim no sympathy.

The jury, obediently, found her guilty, and the judge, describing her crime as one of the most horrible in the history of the world, sentenced her to die on the last day of August.

The prisoner now suddenly began to do her own keening, as a contemporary account tells:

The prisoner sat down as soon as the sentence was pronounced and commenced to cry aloud, rocking herself to and fro and uttering screams that could be heard far beyond the court house. After some delay she was removed, still screaming, from the court house and carried to the jail, where for some time she continued to utter screams that were heard by the crowd without.

This screaming episode added to the bizarre drawing power Bridget Durgan seemed to have while in jail. A woman who was so plain that earlier employers, when questioned, genuinely could not describe what she had looked like, and who had made less than no impact on dozens of homes through which she had passed, scrubbing and cooking, was now a major attraction. Just as people at the time visited what were called lunatic asylums, to amuse themselves and scare their children by watching the behaviour of unhinged inmates, so respectable middle-class Americans on the east coast could not let that summer go by without a visit to view Bridget Durgan. It is difficult to imagine the confusion and indignity of the woman from Sligo as she daily faced, through the bars of her cell, a stream of elegantly clad censorious and curious watchers.

The hanging had even more drawing power, in spite of the fact that decency had begun to operate in relation to executions, which were no longer positioned as events of public entertainment, surrounded by thousands of viewers, chomping on food proffered by street vendors, and beguiled, before and after the main event, by singers and poets rhyming off ballads about the criminal executed on that particular day.

That was no longer the case, and so Bridget might have expected a private hanging. There were, of course, some tickets in the gift of the sheriff, and these were eagerly sought after. It seems that the sheriff was a man who could not give "No" for an answer, for on the day that Bridget died, the prison compound was filled to bursting point with almost 2000 guests, some of them having achieved entry by having themselves sworn in as temporary deputies.

It was a hot day, that 31 August, and the crowds could not be contained in the prison compound. Some favoured women got places at the upper windows of the jail, overlooking the *hoi polloi*. Some of the men climbed onto the roof of a nearby barn, where they were just slightly above the level of the roof of the prison, and so could see what happened on the gallows. Private enterprise even created a tall platform outside the prison to accommodate those who could neither get into the prison compound nor up onto the barn roof, and this platform got so much custom that it collapsed under the weight of the would-be spectators.

"The roughest, rudest, and most ungentlemanly crowd of men we ever saw," was how the *New York Times* described the gathering. "Many hundreds of profane, indecent and ungentlemanly persons . . . pushed, and hauled and swore and fought. Every man pushed for position. Oaths and profane ejaculations of the most outrageous nature mingled with cries and calls, such as one may hear at a circus. For five minutes, we stood in the midst of these brutes and wondered of what stuff and refuse they were made."

It would have created something of a late-onset heroic counterpoint if Bridget Durgan had arrived at the place of execution in white-faced resolute dignity and died instantly at the hand of an expert.

But if Bridget Durgan's destiny decreed that her life be nasty, brutish and short, it further decided that her death should be nasty, brutish – and long.

Some of the elements of a dignified departure were there, all right. There were two priests present. Bridget was dressed in a plain brown suit with a white collar, and her callused working woman's hands were untypically encased in gloves. But at that point, dignity ended, for the condemned woman was so drunk as she came to her place of punishment that she could not walk, and was effectively supported by the two priests sent to minister to her. Nor was the drunkenness of her own choosing. The authorities apparently made the decision that they didn't want her either repeating the screaming episode or falling down in one of her frequent seizures, and opted instead to have her anaesthetised with alcohol. They woke her at around five in the morning and fed her neat alcohol for some hours.

Although they got her standing on the scaffold, how long that stance could be held by a grossly intoxicated, terrified and confused woman was questionable, so the procedures were run through in a tawdry scramble. The cap was fitted over Bridget's head. Now she was ready for the final insult.

The normal executioner, unlike the judge, did not see Bridget as having been "unsexed" by her crime, and, since he normally hanged only men, he refused to kill her. Amateurs were brought in for that purpose, and they reversed the usual process. Instead of rigging a trapdoor which would fall away from beneath the condemned woman's feet, dropping her to the end of the rope which, if correctly positioned, would dislocate her spinal cord and cause virtually instantaneous death, these amateurs rigged a system of weights, which, when released, saw the woman dragged three feet off the ground by the noose, to be held there, in full view of the appreciative crowds, while she slowly died of strangulation, kicking and contorting for many minutes.

This, the nauseated *New York Times* reporter claimed,

"afforded amplest gratification" to the watching crowd.

Then, the moneymaking started. The two priests who had attended Bridget said nothing. No priest ever gives to the public the contents of confessions made to him. Yet confessions surfaced for sale in the direct aftermath of the execution. One of them seemed to be particularly good value for the ghoulish, because it was, its purveyors claimed, written by the dead woman herself. This fraudulent claim could not have been true, since Bridget was, to the day of her ghastly death, completely illiterate.

The confessions varied in their detail, but were uniform in their effect, which was to justify the verdict and the execution and to crystallise the public perception of the domestic servant as sub-human, and therefore deserving of neither sympathy nor second thoughts. Some claimed that she had planned the murder for weeks. Some suggested that the deed was done to eliminate the doctor's wife and allow Bridget to take her place. And one came with its own commentary, which suggested that the main problem was that Bridget did not "know her place."

"That she was exceedingly ambitious is beyond all manner of doubt," wrote the commentator disapprovingly. "That she constantly endeavoured to rise above her condition is equally certain."

What is significant about this judgement is that it provides a contemporaneously satisfying reason why Durgan's crime led her to the gallows, whereas Lizzie Borden's merely put her into the anthologies of children's rhymes.

Lizzie Borden, according to those rhyming anthologies, took an axe, and with it "gave her father forty whacks/When she saw what she had done/She gave her mother forty-one."

It was a neat singsong summary of a crime of stark brutality and frenzied violence. Yet Lizzie Borden was helped by precisely the same prejudices and assumptions that dragged Bridget Durgan to the end of the amateur executioner's rope.

Lizzie Borden didn't *look* like a murderer. Bridget Durgan did. Lizzie Borden was middle class and elegantly dressed. Bridget Durgan was a clumsily-dressed peasant. Lizzie Borden was well connected. (Although most criminologists today believe that she eliminated at least two of those connections: her mother and her father, in a murderous attack.) Bridget Durgan may not have literally been an orphan, but she seems to have been cast loose from family and friends. Lizzie Borden fitted the stereotype of a lady to be protected. Bridget Durgan fitted the stereotype of a sub-human, animal-like horror figure to be scotched. Lizzie Borden was a competent businesswoman who seems to have been ambitious to run her own life and own her own property. Bridget Durgan's embryonic aspirations to any kind of control over her own shattered life seem to have been regarded almost as a hanging matter in themselves.

"So the way was clear to treat her as the public mind wished: to make of her a summary example for all rebellious servants," sums up Ann Jones. "And most people seemed quite able either to disregard the very real mitigating circumstances of her poverty and sickness or to consider them only as further evidence of her brutish, subhuman nature."

DEATH BY DROWNING IN FOUR INCHES OF WATER

A Murder in Connemara

Ireland has always been a great place for gossip. These days, columnists in newspapers get well paid for it, as long as it's about the relatively rich and relatively famous.

The bulk of gossip has always been free, however, and has covered the lives of people who are *not* household names. Brinsley McNamara immortalised the toxic influence of gossip in his novel, *The Valley of the Squinting Windows*, but he ignored the function gossip fulfils in bringing to justice those who might otherwise evade it. Gossip has served this function more than once in relation to murder.

A classic case was the death of "Sonny" Dan Walsh, a farmer in his fifties living not far from Patrick Pearse's summer cottage in Rosmuc, Connemara. "Sonny" was found face-down in four inches of water in a little stream, quite close to a small wooden bridge. The water had covered his mouth and nose, and he was dead when the gardaí arrived on the scene. A post-mortem revealed injuries on the dead man's head; injuries so minor that the general view was that "Sonny" might have been stunned, but certainly not knocked unconscious. Small marks on his

196

face seemed to have been caused by pebbles in the stream.

"'Sonny" Dan's widow, Annie, confirmed that on the Wednesday of his death, 30 May 1928, her husband had been working hard on the farm all day, had come home to eat his supper and put the younger children to bed, and had then gone back out, to travel to Oughterard in order to have a crib made. She had given him one pound and ten shillings to pay for the crib, and had heard no more of him until notified, on the following day, of his death.

"I find that the said Dan Walsh died from asphyxia due to accidental drowning," announced the coroner, ending a sad story.

Except that the sad story wanted to go on being told, and it found its way into gossip around the dead man's home village and nearby townlands. The central figure in the gossip was his widow, Annie. This was Annie's second experience of widowhood. She had been married in the USA in 1914 to a man who died four years later, after which she returned to Ireland, together with three daughters, and married "Sonny" Dan, by whom she had two sons and a daughter. But in recent years, the gossip said, she had been seeing a much younger man, and seeing him in her own home, at that.

The younger man, Martin Joyce, was from Rosmuc. He often came to the Walshes' house and played cards or shared general crack there, remaining after most of the other visitors had left, and more than once leaving in the early hours of the following morning. *Dúirt bean liom go ndúirt bean léi* that Annie Walsh often took part in the card games and crack, while her much quieter husband put the children to bed and went off to bed early himself, sleeping in the same room as the youngest child.

The whispers grew in volume, and the theories grew with them. Now some of the whisperers were not satisfied that "Sonny" Dan had died the way the coroner thought he had died. Some of the whisperers even suggested that a death potion of some kind had been mixed for the quiet farmer, in order to take him out of what was shaping up to be a triangle which, if not eternal, was likely to last too long for Annie's patience.

After about six months, enough of these rumours had reached the ears of the local gardaí to make them worried enough to notify headquarters. In due course a team of gardaí which included some men who later became legends in investigative work, headed for Connemara, and, not long after their arrival there, the decision was made to exhume the body of "Sonny" Dan Walsh. On 28 November of the year he died, "Sonny" Dan Walsh's body emerged from its grave, and the State Pathologist went to work on it. He failed to find signs of poisoning, and indicated that there simply wasn't enough evidence to allow him to form an opinion on any particular cause of death.

So the gardaí were in a pickle. On the one hand, they had a large number of people who were angrily convinced that a quiet man had been done to death by his wife – or on behalf of his wife – because of her illicit relationship with a younger man. On the other hand, they had no particular evidence to point to anything other than accident as a reason for the farmer's death.

There certainly seemed to be evidence to suggest that an accident had happened to a man who, since he was severely burned in a childhood accident, was regarded as "a bit simple," and who was known to drink a bit. On a short-cut home from Oughterard, it was certainly possible that he had slipped on the boulders at the edge of the water and fallen so heavily into the stream that he had managed to drown in four inches of cold water.

But there were little discrepancies. Little discrepancies like the bottle of poitín. A bottle of good poitín, found in the dead man's pocket. At that time, a bottle of poitín cost about five shillings.

Fair enough. According to the dead man's widow, he had left their home with much more than five shillings. In fact, he had been in possession of one pound and ten shillings. The gardaí went to work to find who had sold him the poitín (a difficult task at any time), who he had been drinking with, and whether he had paid over the money for the crib.

But the gardaí were also pursuing other lines of inquiry. Assuming, even for a moment, that "Sonny" Dan had died violently, rather than by accident, it was desirable to clear Martin Joyce, the widow's putative boyfriend, by working out precisely where he had been between the time "Sonny" Dan left his own house and the time he was found, dead. Martin Joyce, surprisingly, since it was now six months later, was able to remember in great detail his movements for the whole of the fatal night. There had been a funeral on that day, he told the gardaí, in Inis Mór (the biggest of the three Aran Islands) and he had not only attended, but had done some heavy-duty drinking. He then retraced his steps for the investigators, naming this place where he had taken a boat, this place where he had landed it, this place where he had slept in the open that night, and this other place where he had a cup of tea the following morning. He told the gardaí that he had not got back to his home place until the afternoon of the day that "Sonny" Dan's body had been found. All of this impressive detail had only one drawback to it. Nobody could be found to corroborate any of it. Martin Joyce had been AWOL for more than twelve hours on the night of the murder, as far as any of his friends or acquaintances knew. On the other hand, one person had seen Martin Joyce on that night, and was happy to confirm the sighting to the gardaí.

This witness was a nephew of the murdered man, and he had seen Martin Joyce on the brightly moonlit night of the murder, at around eleven o'clock, because his dog had barked, and he had got out of bed to quiet the animal and had, glancing out of the window, spotted his uncle and Martin Joyce going past.

None of which added up to an impregnable case for the gardaí, but on the other hand, the rumour machine was rolling again, and this time the message was a threatening one for the gardaí; young Joyce was in the process of packing his bags and heading for Canada. The possibility that he might flee forced the gardaí to move faster. Statements were taken and checked against each other. The pace heated up. People began to make mistakes. Not garda personnel; survivors. Particularly the widow, whose statement said she had never been out of the house on the night of the murder. When this was matched with a statement taken from her fourteen-year-old daughter Mary (who was born during Annie's first, American marriage), it could be shown that Mary disagreed. Annie *had* been out of the house on that night. Annie now took unilateral action, sending her ten-year-old daughter Rita to the Aran Islands. Out of harm's way. And out of the gardaí's way. Or so she thought. In fact, what happened was that she had put Rita out of her circle of control and so, when the gardaí tracked the girl down on the Aran Islands, she talked freely to them and agreed that Martin Joyce had certainly been in the house the night of the murder. Not so, her mother's statement had claimed.

While some of the investigators were on the Aran Islands, some were nearer home, talking to locals who had been regular guests at the Walsh home.

One of those locals told them that on the evenings when "Sonny" Dan had gone off to bed, his wife Annie had sat beside Martin Joyce, and the two of them had made jokes at the older man's expense.

Annie could feel the questioning closing in around her, and she continued to make mistakes in her attempt to rectify earlier mistakes, admitting that Martin Joyce had in fact been in her house the night of the murder. At the same time, she began to be frantic in her efforts to shut her daughters up, realising that as each gave honest statements to the gardaí, the investigators were, item by item, hint by hint, discrepancy by discrepancy, building up a case against her and against Martin Joyce. One of her daughters later said that her mother had beaten her after the murder and made her promise to tell a particular series of lies to the gardaí.

As Annie was becoming more and more unsure, the gardaí were becoming more and more certain. They took further statements from the teenage daughters, and built the story up for themselves.

It went like this.

Martin Joyce, very drunk, had called to the Walsh house on the afternoon of the murder and spent the afternoon with Annie. That night, the three members of the triangle sat in front of the fire, Joyce with a bottle of poitín. Later on, Joyce and Walsh had left the house and were followed by Annie. The next time Joyce and Annie were seen in the house was in the very early morning, when one of the daughters noticed that the footwear of both mother and younger man were muddy and wet.

Thereafter, Joyce disappeared until the funeral, after which he stayed in the house for three weeks, hiding in the attic during the daytime and climbing down at night.

The plan, apparently, was for Martin Joyce and Annie Walsh to get quickly married. A family departure for Canada was then planned, with the twenty-five-year-old Joyce suddenly becoming stepfather to six children, three of them the offspring of "Sonny" Dan. This would not have been a complete surprise to the children, because apparently some softening-up process had already been undertaken by Annie, who had, earlier on, pondered the possibilities of "Sonny" Dan dying and Martin Joyce living with them instead, seeking the children's approval of this hypothesis. It also emerged that Annie had dosed "Sonny" Dan with artificial manure added to his tea, believing it was a lethal poison. Her husband had survived this, although he had complained about the taste of the tea.

Both Annie Walsh and Martin Joyce were accused of murder and appeared at Green Street Central Criminal Court on 18 June 1929, where a trial, with all the evidence given in Irish, was conducted. Witness after witness spoke of theatrical threats being made against individuals who were spreading rumours about Annie and Martin – she had promised to throw boiling water over them – and of similar threats made against "Sonny" Dan.

When it came to the time to sum up, the judge said he wanted to say a special word of recognition of the effort the jury had made to concentrate on the case. (It can't have been easy, with the barristers arguing in English, and the liveliest of testimony being delivered *as Gaeilge*.

He then went on to refer to the "intrigue" which, it was alleged, was going on between Joyce and Annie Walsh. That, he told the jury, was a matter which should not enter their consideration of the question of whether or not both the accused or either of them had been guilty of the crime of murder. It had been urged that the unfortunate man, being partly drunk, slipped on the rocks and fell into the stream and was drowned in three or four inches of water. To do that would almost suggest a suicide, seeing that there was no trace of a struggle . . . had the body been placed in such a way as to suggest that it was an accident? What had become of the thirty shillings the dead man was proved to have had with him when he left his home?

His lordship went on to point to the significance of the daughter's evidence that her mother's dress had been "draggled and soiled" even though the mother had said she had not been out of the house that night. The judge also quoted an observation Martin Joyce had made when asked about the crime.

"What can they say to me," he had asked rhetorically, "when they did not see me do it?"

The jury considered for an hour and three quarters before returning a verdict of guilty on both of the accused.

When asked if he had anything to say, Martin Joyce was mute. He looked as if he wanted to speak, but no words issued from him. After a pause, the judge then donned the black cap and sentenced the young man to die on 18 July.

Annie Walsh was then brought forward, and in what the *Irish Independent* of the following day described as "a scene of the most tense excitement," insisted on telling the court that she was not guilty. The judge sentenced her to die on the same day as her lover and told her that he totally approved of the verdict of the jury.

Joyce's aged father, who had attended the trial from the beginning, broke down and had to be assisted, weeping, from the courthouse.

The prisoners were then removed. Up to that point, Annie Walsh stood straight in the dock and betrayed no emotion. Martin Joyce, who had already looked heartsick, as he was being removed from the dock after sentence uttered what one of the detectives later described as "an unmerciful roar which struck terror into all those in court."

The death sentences were later reprieved, and Martin Joyce and Annie Walsh served life sentences for the murder of the man they had jeered at during card games.

Bibliography

Jones, Ann, *Woman Who Kill*, New York: Fawcett Crest, 1980.

Kennedy, Ludovic, *10 Rillington Place*, Victor Gollancz, 1974.

Miller, Kerby A., *Emigrants and Exiles: Ireland and the Irish Exodus to North America*, Oxford: Oxford University Press, 1985.

Norris, Joel, *Serial Killers*, Anchor Books, Doubleday, 1988.

O'Brien, Sean, *Bloody Ambassadors*, Dublin: Poolbeg, 1993.

Torrey, E Fuller, MD, *Surviving Schizophrenia: A Family Manual*, New York: Harper and Row, 1988.

Pierrepoint, Albert, *Pierrepoint: Executioner*, London: Harrap, 1974.

Prone, Terry, *Irish Murders* (1) *The Shocking True Stories*, Dublin: Poolbeg, 1992.

Sifakis, Carl, ed., *The Encyclopaedia of American Crime*, Smithmark, 1982.

Also by Poolbeg

Irish Murders 1

by

Terry Prone

Irish Murders 1 is a startling, comprehensive, shivers-up-the-spine read with pictures of the killers and the locations in which the celebrated murders took place. It is based on wide-ranging research and scores of interviews.

Bestselling writer Terry Prone here tells the savage stories of real-life murders – recent and not so recent – in Ireland: the shocking details of death and destruction; the painstaking work of the detectives; the confessions; the court cases; the suicides. They're all here, including:

The case of Nurse Mamie Cadden, abortionist, and the two dead bodies of clients found on her doorstep.

The double murder by Malcolm Macarthur that cost an Attorney General his job and helped to bring down a government.

The prostitute strangled on Sandymount Strand, still wearing the bracelet she had bought as a pilgrim to Lourdes.

The bizarre story of the two Irish men who had a special line in serial killing.

The tragedy of sixteen-year-old Hazel Mullen, killed and dismembered by medical student Shan Mohangi in the basement of The Green Tureen restaurant in Harcourt Street, Dublin.